Appreciation

What Every Woman Still Needs

Ruth McRoberts Ward

BAKER BOOK HOUSE
Grand Rapids, Michigan 49516

Original art by Dean Vavak.

Copyright © 1981 by Baker Books
a division of Baker Book House Company
P.O. Box 6287, Grand Rapids, MI 49516-6287

Trade-size edition, February 1989

ISBN: 0-8010-9697-9

Second printing, October 1995

Printed in the United States of America

*To my husband Jim, who
communicates appreciation*

Contents

Foreword

Marriage is changing. And the changes are causing trouble.

If the present rate of divorce continues for a generation, two out of every five couples now married will end up in the divorce court. Of those who remarry after divorce, more than two out of five will experience another breakup. Divorce is painful for those involved—for the man and woman, and for their children. Surely all this pain and distress isn't necessary. But what can be done about it?

In this book Ruth Ward clearly and convincingly describes two solutions. First, we need to understand what is happening to marriage in our rapidly changing modern world. We no longer travel on horses but in automobiles and in airplanes. We no longer light our homes with candles, but with electricity. Equally dramatic changes have taken place in marriage relationships.

In our democratic society the *companionship marriage* has largely replaced the traditional marriage, in which the husband is boss. Marriage is no longer a one-vote system but a two-vote system, in which both partners must reach agreement if they are to live together in harmony.

Once we understand what makes a good marriage relationship, we need to put our understanding into action. To use an automobile instead of a horse, we have to understand a very complex piece of machinery. To replace candles with modern lighting, we have to know how to deal with electricity. And to achieve a truly satisfying companionship marriage, we have to learn the rules for managing close relationships. Ruth Ward offers guidelines in this book that could make all the difference between success and failure in marriage.

Above all else, we must recognize two basic principles. First, for a happy marriage husband and wife must communicate with each other, openly and honestly, about their inner feelings, thoughts, wishes, and intentions.

Second, in order to keep a marriage working smoothly, husband and wife must affirm and keep on affirming each other. They must offer appreciation and support, and give to each other a continuing sense of worth.

Do these things and keep on doing them in your marriage, and all will be well. Fail to do them, and you will run into trouble sooner or later. That is the message of this book, which Ruth Ward makes come alive again and again by quoting couple after couple whom she knows personally or with whom she has worked in a counseling relationship. As we turn the pages, these people offer us their own experiences of success and of failure to underscore the message.

We know Ruth Ward and her husband Jim personally. They are dynamic and dedicated people, and it is out of their personal experience that this book has been written. May its message help to increase the number of happy marriages in today's world!

David and Vera Mace

Introduction

Effective communication in marriage is what this book is all about. Some couples live together for years and never reveal their real selves. Some spouses are reluctant to divulge their intimate feelings, desires, and needs for fear that they will be misunderstood or rejected. Other mates, willing to share and listen, just need assistance in learning how.

When I first shared with friends the title for this book, women responded with deep sighs of relief and gave encouragements like: "It's about time! How long will it take?"; "Oh, good! I'll buy a copy for Bill"; "This is what I've been needing"; and "My husband needs to read it; he thinks I'm automatic pilot."

Most of the men, however, shot me bewildered, if not jealous looks, and whined, "But, what about me? I need to be appreciated, too."

"That's true," I assured them. "A husband desperately needs his wife's encouragement to supplement and draw out his potential strengths of leadership. A wife who understands that principle and uses her God-given ability to encourage, has a richer, more fulfilling marriage, one that grows and flourishes. Both partners realize personal worth."

Just as men yearn for and respond to encouragement, women hunger for appreciation. It surprises some men that women even need any kind of encouragement because they seem to operate very well without it. "After all," I've heard some men say, "they have the children who need them and hang on to every word they say." Others have defended their neglect by saying, "She seems very happy with running around, her job, and taking care of the house."

Women—single and married—are hurting. They blame marriage, husbands, children, parents, and circumstances. But the majority want solutions rather than sympathy.

Most women are struggling to adjust to modern female role changes without ignoring or threatening the masculine ego—an endeavor that takes nearly as much skill as walking a tightrope.

Paul Tournier, in *A Place for You* (Harper and Row) says, "Gentlemen reflect smugly that there are more women than men in the psychotherapist's consulting room. But we often have the impression that it is the husband who ought to be consulting us, because the wife is not finding in him the support she needs, and that is what is making her ill."

When women learn that their hungers for appreciation are not unique, but shared by millions of other wives, they relax and determine to adjust.

Appreciation, synonymous with love, is so vital to women, that husbands must make it their daily concern. Appreciation is an umbrella term covering many intricate and intimate areas.

This book is addressed to women with the hope that they will pass on bits and pieces to their husbands. It is my desire to help women identify their needs and interpret them to their spouses.

I have changed all names and situations in the accounts of personal experiences for confidentiality.

The sketches by Dean Vavak are meant to be handy hooks for remembering the various aspects and applications of appreciation. Just as oil and grease are vital to automotive function, appreciation smooths the rough spots in a marriage.

Ruth Ward
York, Pa.

1

Expansion of Women's Roles

We are in the throes of a female revolution. I prefer to call it expansion of female roles. Much of the traditional lifestyle of the 1940s is gradually diminishing as women postpone marriage and/or having children, in lieu of education, employment, or careers. Many women prefer to defer marriage until they can be reasonably assured of a fail-safe choice of mate.

New concepts like househusband, working mothers, open marriage, feminist movement, single parent, homosexuality, and female executive which accompany this expansion of roles not only challenge our security but threaten to uproot our traditional lifestyles. Every family is affected in some way. Especially burdened and concerned with the changes are people who were reared in the slower paced and secure 1930s and 40s.

In bygone days, a woman was expected to marry

15

soon after high school graduation, have a family, and depend on her husband's decisions and financial support. Only if one went unclaimed or chose a religious career was she socially free to enter the man's world, support herself, and make her own decisions. Very few women mixed career and marriage. Only providentially childless women or wealthy women, who could afford hired child care, were physically and psychologically free to develop their personal potential by getting involved with business, politics, or community affairs.

Since the majority of couples had large families and few modern conveniences, the mother's week was consumed by survival. The lyrics to a song we used to sing recapture the secure and presumably happy atmosphere of the locked-in lifestyle.

> Today is Monday, Monday, washday.
> Everybody happy?
> Well, I must say.
>
> Today is Tuesday, Tuesday, ironing day.
> Everybody happy?
> Well, I must say.
>
> Wednesday was mending day,
> Thursday was baking day,
> and Friday was cleaning day.

A woman with six or seven kids—or fourteen in some cases—was on duty until her mid-fifties, always having a little one at home to keep her from being lonely. Married children, often living next door or on the next farm, prolonged the mother's sense

of worth by depending on her assistance as a grandmother. These women never ran out of things to do. In fact, women were so domestically involved, they hardly had time to wonder if they were happy as individuals. They just assumed they were.

Anne Morrow Lindbergh, in *Gift from the Sea* (Random House, 1975) says, "Woman wants perpetually to spill herself away. All her instinct as a woman—the eternal nourisher of men, of society— demands that she give."

Achieving for the family's welfare largely fed the woman's need for appreciation. She was always busy making quilts, grape juice, pretty doilies, ice cream, new clothing, jam, sweaters, and candy, canning fruits and vegetables, and providing medical care. The ohs and ahs from children and husband encouraged her to keep up the good work.

But now, men and women alike are challenging many of the traditional limitations of female roles. Note the attitudes illustrated by the following children's interview of bygone days:

> "What do you want to be when you grow up?" a little girl was asked. "A nurse, or maybe a teacher; probably a mother," came her traditional reply.
> "What would you like to be if you were a little boy?"
> "Oh, then, I could be anything I wanted," she said brightly.

When little boys were asked the same questions, most of them gave the usual list—fireman, policeman, pilot, or doctor. When asked, "If you were a girl, what do you think you'd like to be when you grew up?" one of the boys shrugged, "In that case, I guess I'd grow up to be nothing." This interview expresses many women's objections to being female.

Our nation is adjusting to the female revolution whether we like it or not, because girls like the idea of choosing to do what interests them most rather than following a stereotyped female pattern. Women—rich, poor, educated and uneducated, professional and nonprofessional, married and single—for the first time in history, are emerging en masse out of the domestic cocoon. This trek agrees with some, but is harmful for others. When the woman changes, the home changes and the world changes. We must try to understand so that we can make wise adjustments.

Where Have all the Mothers Gone?

What has brought on this change? The Equal Rights Amendment? No! This is a result of something much bigger: progress. Commodities, convenience, and technology to a great extent have necessitated and encouraged our nation to migrate from country to city. Many women have more leisure time than they want. Inflation has made it necessary for many women to take on jobs to help support their families. It is easy to understand why women have been ushered away from motherhood and the home—some reluctantly and others eagerly—in pursuit of a second check or just for something to do.

19

Years ago the unusual phenomenon was a single woman, a childless couple, or a couple with only one or two children. Now a family consisting of more than three children is not only a marvel but is often frowned on. So the question is not only Where have all the mothers gone? but Where have all the children gone? Because of birth control, business careers, and the rising cost of living, women are not having as many children. This has upset the female psychological cart.

Women's Dilemma

Naturally change produces problems along with progress. Because responsibility of caring for children now ends while a woman is still relatively young and because modern convenience and packaged commodities shorten a mother's work week, women feel unneeded with nothing to do in an empty house all day. As a result, women are struggling for identity and independence. They want to be important enough to choose to do what they believe will satisfy them, whether it is career, business, or singlehood, or the traditional marriage, children, and home route.

They clamor for solid relationships with friends, relatives, spouses, and children. Most of all, they want to be understood and appreciated for who they are and not solely for what they do.

David and Vera Mace say (*Christian Freedom for Women* [Broadman Press]): "Most of the changes have come gradually at first, but their effect has been progressively to shift the focus of community life—the place where the action is—further and further away from home. This has reached its extreme point in the big cities of today, with the family home isolated in the suburbs, and the father away all day, while the children are at school or in kindergarten or occupied in the evening with activities planned for them alone."

With more free time and with an eye on the future, mothers are endeavoring to set and reach intellectual and career goals as well as to take care of households and children. Women's groups encourage a woman to invest her time, abilities, and intelligence.

Tension in the Home

Though all this advancement has made more opportunities for females and challenged and satisfied women's search for identity and self-worth, it has not happened without tragedy, as indicated by the number of marriages ending in divorce. Since the alarming divorce rate in some way affects virtually every home, people are frantic to discover the cause.

Some people blame all our domestic upheaval on the struggle for women's rights, believing the way to end the strife is to go back to the traditional lifestyle.

Others blame the current marriage struggles directly on women who have left the home for whatever reasons to get a job. According to the United States Labor Department, the number of employed married women soared past six million in the 1970s. But other factors than outside work are involved since not only employed women's homes are affected by women's lifestyle changes and divorce. Studies reveal that moving from an agricultural to industrial society, rural to suburbia—a socioeconomic condition—influenced by inflation and progress, has really triggered the trends toward the women's lifestyle revolution. And this is an irreversible situation.

Following are some opinions from men and women I have interviewed regarding women's role changes.

"If they would reduce their standards of living and let their husband's checks support their families, everything would return to normal" (normal being the 1940s).

"Women should leave running of the country and business to men who are equipped to do it."

"We would not have these problems if women stopped trying to be like men."

"Women are never satisfied. Because they are fickle, they cannot handle being out in the world."

"Youth problems with drugs and sex would disappear if women returned home."

"If women would obey God and take a lesser place as the Bible commands, we would return to the stable 40s."

"If wives would be in total submission, this would never happen."

Understanding Women

Most women want neither the passive nor the aggressive role. Women need men and men need women. And women need men to need women. But there are some limits to all this needing lest it become demanded rather than bestowed in love.

David and Vera Mace maintain that marriages break up because of lack of companionship. Lack of communication keeps companionship marriages from happening.

To understand and appreciate the current male-female dilemma, let's discuss some common divorce-prone husband-wife relationships influenced by husbands' varied roles, ranging from babies to kings.

2

Husbands — Babies or Kings?

What Is Happening to Men?

Expansion of women's roles is naturally affecting men, exposing insecurities and fears in many, selfishness and impatience in others, but gentleness, consideration, and encouragement in those who are open-minded and willing to care, listen, and learn.

If females are allowed to be as free as men, some husbands question, what will happen to men? Who will take care of them, cook their meals, buy and wash their clothing, satisfy their need for physical love?

A few men envision total freedom of women as masculine-looking females dressed in bright red uniforms, carrying machine guns and threatening to take over the world. "Let's keep the women in

their place at home," one husband voiced. "Keep them uneducated, barefoot, and pregnant," another said half-jokingly. One well-known male author even suggested that because women are so intelligent and influential, it is best to keep them hemmed in and limited socially lest they get lofty ideas and outshine the men.

Bold, bossy women really frighten men and rightly so. Some men, coming from female dominant homes are actually so intimidated by women's powerful influence, that they choose to be babies.

On the other hand, men from male chauvinistic homes seem almost afraid to encourage their wives at all for fear their wives will take advantage of them. In order to protect their authority, prestige, or personal welfare, they become bold and bossy kings.

To facilitate solution, we will compare these two most common types of husbands which are carry-overs from the 1930s and 40s—and from the first century, believe it or not—with the type that guarantees growth and will best meet the relationship needs of our day.

Mommy-Wives

Some men get married primarily because they want someone to assume their mother's role—wake them, feed them, take care of their belongings, nurse them, keep them from being lonely, and bawl them out when they are late or negligent. Some of these husbands lazily and selfishly allow their wives to do the dirty work and menial tasks. They nearly fall apart when their wives become ill or go away.

Some husbands are actually too lazy to manage the home and find it very comfortable to allow the woman to be in charge. "My wife gives me ten dollars a week spending money," I have heard some men brag or complain.

Many of these men assume that all females like to do the same things. They believe that since their mothers were content to stay home all day that this is the way all women should be. They are appalled to learn that some women don't want children, that many dislike housework and have little interest in baking pies or sewing garments. Modern women courageously resist being mommy-wives even though their mothers may have taught them the traditional role of waiting on men hand and foot, which, by the way, fashions young boys into husbands who resemble demanding infants. Some wives seek employment just to alleviate such a situation.

Because a mommy-wife assumes the bulk of running the home, children, and finances, she often becomes very domineering and treats her mate like another child, talking down to him and ordering him around. This not only destroys the respect children have for their father, but chips away at a man's self-esteem as well.

Because some men choose to be so dependent on their wives, they are often labeled "hen-pecked." Though this set-up doesn't please the majority of husbands or wives, no one seems to know how to change it. No man wants to be henpecked nor does the normal woman want to henpeck her husband.

Many dominant women are frustrated, like my friend Janie, who in desperation said to her husband, "I'll give you four months to become the man of this house and if you aren't by then, I'll divorce you." There is a fine line between encouragement and manipulation.

Some women receive lots of satisfaction from being mommy-wives, especially those who have little else to occupy their minds and time and those who like to be in control. At the same time, as much as men enjoy being pampered, this lifestyle impedes a growing marriage relationship. There is a difference between being a mommy-wife and pampering a husband with loving and thoughtful support and attention. The mommy-wife role lacks the adoration aspect.

Some women usurp or accept the responsibility and decision-making of home and children from some absent, quiet, or busy husbands, thinking they are shielding them from unnecessary hassle and keeping their lives smooth and trouble free at home to balance the secular dog-eat-dog pressures of the world. When a husband allows this to happen, however, giving little physical affection or emotional support, expecting his needs to be met but not giving the needed respect, attention, and appreciation that the wife needs, the marriage relationship goes sour.

Both spouses need to subject themselves to the other in tenderness and humility, assuring each other of acceptance and approval. Usually women find this easier to do than men.

Fortunately, when most men understand that the wife-husband relationship cannot be a carry-over of mother-son, they are quite willing to adjust their attitudes and bear their share of the load. But it takes work to accomplish this change. Use this book as a tool to assist in such a task.

Doormat Wives

The opposite view—husbands as kings—is really the same song, just a different verse. The husband's word is law. He dictates like a Prussian general.

Some wives are doormats by force, others by choice. The former are sometimes noisy martyrs who let off steam by complaining regularly behind their husband's stiff backs to women friends and relatives—often children—about their unfair treatment. Those who choose the doormat roles are like obedient slaves, enduring verbal and even physical abuse and neglect, while quietly taking the blame for every domestic problem.

This male-dominance view, embracing a one-vote home, perhaps eliminates disagreements but it will not strengthen marriage or foster female contentment.

Many gospel preachers sincerely advocate that God intended woman, because she was created second, to be totally subordinate to man, pouring her total personality and abilities into making him successful, comfortable, and number one. Many women agree. They completely overlook the admonition for husbands to love their wives as Christ loved the church. Christlike love is sacrificial, tender, and uplifting. Therefore, men should treat women as equals and not expect to be served. Each mate should desire to meet the needs of the other, both acting in humility.

Doormat Wives by Choice

Husbands are not always to blame. Many wives try to mold an otherwise fair and sharing husband into a dominant role because it is religiously fashionable in some groups. Some of these women who really want to be God-honoring wives, though hiding behind submission, are really subtly dominant, coaching their husbands from the sidelines about what to say, when to say it, what to do, and when to do it. Often she will manage to direct all the "no" decisions to the father and handle the positive decisions herself. This makes the father appear to be more authoritative.

Some doormat-by-choice wives, so desperate to find happiness and resolve problems in communication, become self-condemning and say, "I am the fault of our problems. I should not expect so much attention from my husband. He is very busy with his job. I should be more submissive and stay out of his way. I should be thankful for all I have financially and not try to make him become someone he is not. I need to stay in my place."

These wives say to their husbands, "I won't expect anything from you. Whenever you want me, I'm here. I will take care of your needs and will arrange my schedule to fit yours. My feelings are secondary. I will gather up what crumbs of affection you throw my way and be grateful. When I serve you, I will consider it the same as serving the Lord. Even if you mistreat me, I know God loves me and I can identify with Christ's sufferings."

Many wives with this attitude actually provoke and invite husbands to mistreat them and even strike them.

By admitting all is her fault because she has not been a submissive wife, a wife denies her husband his adult responsibility, causing his self-esteem to disintegrate. He will often turn obsessively to sports, work, drinking, or another woman in search of satisfaction. Though these submissive wives mean well, they hurt themselves in the long run by not allowing their husbands the privilege of encouraging and supporting them as they share in decision making.

Wives who prefer this facade of masculine control, rather than being motivated out of humility may be either lazy or afraid of personal failure. This frustrates men, especially those who want their wives to assume their fair share of the marriage and home load.

According to James Dobson, noted marriage counselor and author, women receive most of their self-esteem from their husband's approval, and a woman can't get that approval unless there is talk and action from the husband. Often a husband will not give appreciation unless and until the wife lets him know what she needs to hear and have done, and then allows him to do it. This quality communication takes time and skill.

Doormats by Force

Only a very insecure man whips a woman into submission or subordination. In a home where a man sets himself up as a tyrant, no one can be happy, not even the man. Marriages patterned after first-century culture are popular today in some religious circles, where a woman's submission is obligatory rather than voluntary. Proponents of this type of husband-wife relationship deny the intelligence, difference, and dignity of the female gender. Many men are actually frustrated because they cannot delegate responsibilities nor are they self-disciplined and wise enough themselves to assume total responsibility for family direction. Some men even believe that their wives' spiritual lives are spin-offs from theirs. The last chapter deals with this aspect.

Misinterpretation of Scripture has led many well meaning people astray and has caused much turmoil, including divorce, because it denies individuality and freedom among persons, and relegates stiff roles to men who may not be qualified or interested in acting a certain way because they are male. The Bible does not impose on us a particular pattern of marriage, just as it does not insist on a single educational philosophy or specific form of government. Our intent here is not to debate biblical issues. *Christian Freedom for Women*, edited by

Harry Hollis (Broadman, 1975), deals adequately with the biblical concept.

Doormat wives—voluntary or forced—are not content. Many husbands live like sheiks, treating their wives like maids and mistresses. Many men and women are unaware of what has destroyed romance. These relationships, however, can be understood, altered, and healed.

Companion Wives

Not all husbands fall into the babies or kings patterns; but many have tinges of one or both in varying degrees. *Encouragement: A Wife's Special Gift* outlines the intermediary stages.

Many marriages—even Christian ones—are uninteresting. Something is drastically wrong. Though the woman usually feels the lack of luster first, she cannot figure out what is wrong and correct the situation alone. The husband goes his way, the wife goes hers. Both may work hard at jobs they enjoy but be disappointed and disillusioned about the joys of matrimony.

"Women yearn for meaningful male companionship, particularly with their husbands. Most men don't know how to give emotional support because the average woman does not understand men well enough to know how to draw from them the support they crave." Paul Tournier says in *A Place for You* (Harper and Row), "A woman has a greater emotional need than a man has, consciously at least, whereas the husband finds it more difficult to express his feelings, even though in doing so he would be giving his wife the support she needs."

Normal women don't want to rule the roost or be enslaved, babied, or idolized. They want no more than to be regarded as mature, intelligent, and sensitive beings as God created them.

How to establish a relationship through understanding and appreciation is the purpose of the rest of this book. Understanding why women are restless comes first.

3

Women Are Restless

Many modern husbands wonder why women who have so much materially and who have more and more freedom are discontent. This unsettledness has put an added tension on marriage relationships, causing many to end in separation and divorce.

Taken for Granted

"I'm lonely," Beverly admitted. "Mark doesn't fuss over me any more. Affection I have to beg for just doesn't satisfy," she continued. "I didn't realize how much I missed attention until I got around the men at work. I'm afraid of what I'm beginning to feel toward other men. I love to go to work and hate to go home. I could quit my job, but it wouldn't solve a thing. What would I do with my time? I don't dare tell Mark what I'm feeling for other men because it would only hurt him. He has no idea that I'm so unhappy because he is satisfied with his life and I'm a good pretender. But something has to change and quick.

"Don't get me wrong, Mark has no other woman. It's just that he doesn't want me until he is through with everything else. Then I'm usually too tired or hurt to want him."

A marriage is on the rocks. Bev knows it, Mark does not. He goes his way and she goes hers. They rarely talk, never argue. She takes care of the house, works a full-time job, disciplines the children, pays the bills, insists on church attendance, maintains contact with his and her relatives, plans the holidays, and hopes that he will accompany her to some of the family and church affairs. She is restless.

Women don't mind taking care of their husbands' domestic needs, but they want to be liberated from being expected to treat husbands as spoiled children and from feeling obligated to manage the home alone just because they are female. Wives want to be understood as persons and to be appreciated for who they are, not just for what they do. Women instinctively like to serve, but they resent being taken for granted.

"Woman instinctively wants to give," Anne Morrow Lindbergh says in *Gift from the Sea*, "yet resents giving herself in small pieces. . . . We do not see the results of our giving as concretely as man does in his work. . . . Except for the child, woman's creation is so often invisible."

This life of keeping the machinery oiled, rather

than satisfying women, eventually depresses most of them as pointed out in the first chapter. Women want to share roles, not have fixed roles.

Though many wives and mothers get jobs, go to school, or further a career in order to satisfy themselves as well as help to fight inflation, many discover quickly that they are not interested in, nor able to, be superwives, handling perfectly both the work world and home world. After having achieved some measure of equality, independence, and identity, they become all the more restless, because they are still hurting—a hurt which only husbands are equipped to help them get over. Women often feel that men could do without them, though they are sure they could not do without their husbands. Women want to be important, though not just utilitarian.

Wives will be psychologically satisfied as their marriages grow into companionship relationships.

Lack of Conversation

"I learn more about Mike when we visit someone or when I listen to a phone conversation," Sue said. "He volunteers nothing nor asks anything about my day or my feelings."

Passing on family, neighborhood, or office gossip and exchanging daily health and financial information is not real communication but shallow chitchat.

Good communication—sharing ideas, feelings, and goals, what women hunger for, is possible only when understanding and appreciation precede it. Half this assignment falls on the husband. Part of

the solution is realizing that the lack of open and honest dialogue is the main obstacle in marriage disturbance.

For instance, many hardworking, faithful husbands like Sue's assume that financial stability and lack of disagreement denotes that good communication exists. Unhappy wives verify, however, that financial security and lack of arguments do not necessarily indicate satisfying relationships. Conversely, silence and security, that which many men love, may actually hinder communication. Effective communication involves a growing understanding and appreciation of the whole person—background, feelings, goals.

Husbands who have not learned the unique dimension of communication often fill the void in their lives with work, recreation, or someone else. Women complaining to Ann Landers about their disgust in playing second fiddle to bowling, hunting, football, a job, or the TV, find that even Ann admits defeat when it comes to turning a self-centered—or naive—man into a sensitive, caring person. She wisely advises wives not to nag or beg for their husbands' company. The root problem is poor or no communication.

Unfortunately, many workaholic men who are failing in communication at home are being unfairly categorized as self-centered, when actually they are eager to succeed financially in order to assure that they will have no marriage problems. They mean well.

Wives are alarmed to discover that they have more success in talking and listening to other men at work and wonder why their own spouses are so closed-mouthed and not as thoughtful or attentive to their needs. Such women fail to realize that a casual at-work, at-your-best friendship is a far cry from the kind of relationship that sharing a check, relatives, children, and a home demands.

As we all know, these job friendships based on daily, honest and open communication and acceptance can develop into love affairs and eventually into second marriages. Ironically, many of these marriages fail, too, as the couples begin to share the stresses of living together and paying bills together. Their previous communication was only possible under nonthreatening conditions.

Wives can master the art of engaging their own husbands in conversation where careful listening is 50 percent of conversing. (*Encouragement: A Wife's Special Gift* offers workable suggestions.) But as mentioned earlier, the good-communication assignment is half the husband's responsibility, too, requiring his acceptance and approval of the wife.

Arriving at understanding and appreciation may quite legitimately entail disagreements, which tend to discourage many men who prefer peace at any cost.

We all know that opposites attract, though opposites do not get along easily. In nearly every marriage combination that I have encountered, I find natural differences to be the main source of friction and drawbacks to understanding and acceptance.

A nontalker chooses a gabby person, and a bubbly personality is attracted to a superserious one. Many partnerships harbor a night person and an early riser, a slow-motioned one and one who chomps at the bit, a positive-prone person and one who thinks negatively. Throw in cultural and sex difference, and it is easy to see why sparks fly. But these individual qualities when blended properly, produce wholeness, strength, and security. Unfortunately, until men talk and listen, accept and give approval, women will be restless.

Religiously Restless

Women whose husbands do not share the same zeal for worship, whether because their jobs prevent their involvement or they just do not see their need, find themselves in a real stressful situation.

These wives do not want to run ahead of their husbands spiritually, yet are not comfortable allowing their children and themselves to suffer spiritual neglect. They feel that religious training is a joint responsibility. Children are usually reluctant to attend church when their father lacks interest. Mom has difficulty offsetting that negative influence.

To say, "God can make your life full and meaningful sounds like such a lie when mine is so unhappy and purposeless," a young mother of teens confided. Like many other women, she has done what she thought was best, innocently substituting church meetings and involvement in place of companionship with her husband. Unfortunately, she has wound up even more restless and frustrated. The last chapter deals with this common malady.

Beaten by Boredom

After the children left home, Connie realized that she and Carson didn't have much of a personal relationship. She looked around for something to do, someone to talk to. He didn't want her butting into his life after all these years. Perhaps she should find a job to keep her involved—find her own happiness, he suggested. "If she's unhappy," Carson declared defensively, "it's all in her head. I provide a good check, a fine home, a second car, and all the freedom she wants. What more can she ask? It's not my fault she's unhappy," he continued. "I'm innocent. I haven't done anything or said anything. I haven't changed since the day we got married."

Carson is right. He has not said or done anything, but that admission, rather than clearing him from guilt, exposes his fault.

Connie, like millions of wives over forty, is desperate for a companionship marriage. Husbands resist being the total source of their wives' happiness, which is only right, but husbands can meet the wives halfway in helping them to find fulfillment.

Until wives learn to interpret their needs without threatening the men's personal freedom, lifestyle, or opinions, they will get no relief or understanding and will remain restless.

In counseling husbands and wives together, it is amazing to me how little couples really know about each other's deep yearnings, feelings, and dissatisfactions. Indepth communication is not possible until people intentionally try to understand from

44

where each is coming and purposely appreciate and consider the other's needs.

The Runaway Wife

In one day, without warning, Bruce Arnold's life fell apart. His young wife was gone. Not only was his heart broken, but tackling housework, cooking, washing, and total care of two preschoolers was a staggering assignment for a father who had stuck strictly to outside duties. Bruce was worried about Cindy and completely baffled about why she had left.

He was further stunned when a close friend urged him to visit a marriage counselor because he was totally unaware of any marital difficulty. But out of despair and desperation, he buried his pride and called for an appointment.

"Her mind must have snapped," Bruce speculated to the counselor. "That's what everyone says. It's not like her to hurt anyone, especially the kids. She's a good mother. I know she loves the children and I thought she loved me. We have had a great marriage."

"Had you argued about anything recently?" the counselor probed. "No, we never argue. In fact, the night before she left, we had a cookout with neighbors. She didn't act mad at me or seem bothered about anything. I can't understand it. This guy she went with is—was—my friend, too. How could she do this? How could he do it? He just went through a divorce, himself, and we were trying to help him adjust to it. He'd better not hurt her. I know how he slammed his wife around. I feel like finishing him off," he threatened.

"I'm sure you feel deep hostility toward Joe, but Cindy had reasons for leaving. Discovering what they are will take some time," the counselor reasoned. "She may not even know what they are herself. But, in the meantime, live as normally as you can and avoid creating new problems."

Bruce dropped his head and shook it in utter disbelief. "If anyone would have said that this would happen to us," he said sadly, "I would have said they were crazy. Everyone has always told us that we had a perfect marriage. I thought so, too."

What happened in Bruce and Cindy's marriage is happening in millions of homes today. The things Bruce discovered could strengthen any marriage relationship and help other people avoid the same mistakes.

Bruce and Cindy Arnold had been married nearly five years. By both working full time, they bought and furnished a suburban split-level, acquired two automobiles, adequately provided for two children, and afforded golfing and bowling supplies and fees. To avoid needing a babysitter, they worked opposite shifts—he during the day and she at night.

Because Cindy had trouble with her nerves, she quit her job a couple of months earlier to relieve that strain. Bruce took an evening job to pay off accumulated bills and to earn vacation money.

After taking care of the children and home for two weeks, Bruce realized what Cindy had been enduring. When he worked two jobs, he not only was not around but could not give her assistance with the children or home. He admitted that even when he worked one job, he did very little to encourage her. They had no recreation time together because he was too tired to go anywhere after his second job. He had fallen into watching television every night. She was bored with her life though she was busy as a mother.

Cindy and Bruce had married for the right reasons and everything had fallen into place for them as they gathered possessions, gained financial security, and started a family. But their marriage was not growing. They had reached initial goals, but had set no new ones.

By the time a couple has lived together five or six years, they know each other well enough that they tend to take the other for granted. Bruce, content with earning a good pay check and coming home to a wife, children, clean house, and dinner on the table, had settled down. He was satisfied.

Cindy, on the other hand, outwardly happy with her financial security and a husband for which other wives envied her, was extremely busy—resentfully confined—with child care, housework, and an absent husband. She assumed that the lack of excitement and luster in her life must certainly mean that her love for Bruce had died.

Since feelings for a spouse may lose some tingle and excitement because of familiarity, a couple must school themselves in the reality that true love is based on trust. The routine of child and home care plus jobs needs to be blended with plenty of adult companionship and quality time with each other.

Bruce and Cindy had not learned how to communicate. He was unaware that she needed encouragement, attention, approval, and assistance. Neither had they learned the art of indepth sharing but assumed that lack of argument guaranteed good communication.

Bruce learned that failure to disagree for the sake of peace-keeping is not a virtue but a denial of male responsibility, robbing a marriage of the dimension of good communication that open, honest discussion provides.

Bruce was naive as Cindy was as to what makes a companionship marriage—the wife encouraging her husband and the husband appreciating his wife.

Lack of companionship in marriage plagues all types of couples: middle-class; poor; old; childless; professional—including ministers; blue-collar; and even retired couples, who discover much to their surprise, after spending a lifetime together, that they share only material things, relatives, and health problems. Even couples with personal relationships with God and active church affiliation may have difficulties.

Women, young and old, are restless inside the home, outside the home, spiritually, and in their marriage relationship more so than men. Who is going to help them?

"Gentlemen reflect smugly that there are more women than men in the psychotherapist's consulting room. But we often have the impression that it is the husband who ought to be consulting us because the wife is not finding in him the support she needs and that is what is making her ill," so says Paul Tournier in *A Place for You.* "The support we need most is not that which carries us, but that which enables us to leap forward on our own."

Women's needs fall under the umbrella term *appreciation,* which covers many intricate areas.

The following chapters outline the type of attention a woman craves from her husband and also offer suggestions on how to cultivate understanding and appreciation that lead to supportive communication.

While most women do not qualify as powderpuff mechanics, they are aware that an automobile engine needs grease and oil to function properly. I've chosen that illustration to point up the important place appreciation has in a marriage. As oil serves as a lubricant to reduce friction in an engine, appreciation serves as a smoothing agent in a marriage.

4

Assuring Importance

A wife has to be number-one with her husband, before his mother and family and ahead of his job, hobby, or sports. And certainly a wife must be more important than money.

Competing With Money

Because a woman puts the importance of persons ahead of money, she resists and resents a man's preoccupation with and concern over finances. A man, however, looks at success, possessions, and wealth differently than women do. Paul Tournier says in *A Place for You*, "A man draws considerable strength from the interest he has in things, while a woman is interested in things to the extent that she feels that a person is interested in her."

Phyllis and Frank Jones have been married a

little over a year and seem to be agreeing on every subject except financial matters.

"I just don't think Frank is really committed to me," Phyllis complained, "because he refuses to put all our money together. Naturally, he makes more than I do and brought more into the marriage than I did, but when I entrust everything I have to him, shouldn't he give everything he has to me, too, even though he possesses much more?"

This problem surfaces in many second marriages today, as well as in postponed marriages. Sometimes, it is the woman who has acquired some wealth. Communication about financial concerns is one of the chief problem areas in any marriage relationship whether there is little or much money involved. Consequently, in companionships where financial input is lopsided, even more open, honest discussion is a must if the marriage relationship is to survive and grow.

Though it appeared to Frank that Phyllis was struggling for financial equality, the problem was deeper than that. Phyllis needs to know that she is of utmost importance to her husband.

Frank needs to understand Phyllis's deep-seated hunger to be of vast importance in his life. Accepting her as an equal in his tightly-watched financial dealings meets with hostility on his part. Compromise is in order, but getting there requires honest and tactful sharing through conversation. Let's listen.

"I don't agree that financial equality has anything to do with my personal commitment and respect for you, Phyllis," Frank defended. "I'm quite willing to pay the big bills out of my money and you can pay the smaller household bills out of your account, which I will guarantee will always have a good balance. But I have to retain financial control."

"I want to be more important to you than all your money," Phyllis whined. "And unless you're willing to give me all you have, I don't have but part of you." She paused. "You're more important to me, Frank, than all my money," Phyllis said tearfully.

Like most men, Frank derives the bulk of his security from financial success, which he guards carefully.

"I don't mind contributing a significant amount to the household account which I want you to have freedom to control," he said. "But to demand that you have equal access and approval of how I handle the money saved years before we even met, I consider to be an unreasonable request," he argued.

A stalemate had been reached, it seemed. But when Phyllis understood the different sources of security for men and women, she backed down with her request. She realized that generally women find it easier and more natural to give everything, even out of poverty—like the widow and her two mites—because their security lies primarily in people rather than in possessions, and that men put their chief trust in financial security.

Psychologists confirm that men are more likely to suffer deep depression, even to the point of ending their lives, after loss of job, position, or health, more so than from domestic problems, while most women can endure almost any problem better than a relationship failure. In short, a woman wants to be most important to a man while a man considers being financially secure of first importance.

When a couple begins their companionship on the same limited financial base, this problem is less likely to occur. In marriage where the husband is older and already established financially, like Frank, or where a postponed marriage allows one or both to accumulate wealth and property, these concerns will have to be thoroughly talked through and tenderly worked out.

Sometimes when the tables are turned and the woman brings financial security into the marriage, the husband often feels very helpless, threatened by his wife's financial independence—the very thing he wants to provide. I have observed more than one man destroying or using up a wife's money in order to establish equality.

Women like Phyllis go to great lengths and suffer much emotional turmoil as they struggle to convert their husbands to their point of view. But intimate sharing of feelings is the only way to break the impasse.

The Jones's first step was to be open about how each one looked at the disagreement and the emotional problems that it exposed. Phyllis had in her mind that a joint account was the only way couples who trusted each other should operate. Many couples, however, choose to carry separate accounts not only to allow each one to have a sense of independence and to keep both spouses on their toes financially, but to have established credit with a bank.

54

Frank wanted Phyllis to have a sense of independence in the responsibility of bill paying, but since it was better business procedure to keep his investments and large debts separate from other bills, he preferred to continue with his original accounting and financial planning system.

Phyllis finally realized it was unreasonable to expect Frank to accept her opinion that total trust had to be based on financial equality, feeling that unless he was willing to pool all their money, he was holding out on her and displaying a form of distrust. When she understood that the intensity of Frank's need to retain major control of his investments and financial concerns formed the very base of his security and paralleled her own need to be number-one with him, she realized that to ask him to relinquish control would be like his asking her to play second fiddle to his mother.

One compromise that Phyllis and Frank made was to open their separate accounts to each other's scrutiny and to be accountable to each other. This satisfied Phyllis's curiosity concerning the big black account book. Frank also agreed to jointly tithe their income. When a man is faithful to the Lord financially and trusts God enough to tithe his total income—large or small—a wife will soon develop a strong and stable trust in that man.

Vying for Prime Time

"Ronnie has been a faithful mate and dependable husband for fifteen years," Julie shared. "He encouraged me through secretarial school and into a good accounting business. He has provided adequately for our three children. Although we are both Christians, I'm much more church involved. But I'm not happy. Something is missing.

"Ronnie and I just don't have any fun. There's no time for it for one thing. He brings work home every night. By the time I handle chauffeuring the kids, supervising homework, dinner, and so on, it's late. I don't think he even minds that we never talk, go places together, or laugh any more.

"He plays golf every weekend with his buddies. I wait for him to come home, wait for him to get rested, then wait until he watches his favorite TV show. By then, there's no time left for us, or I'm so tired that I don't care if we have time together or not.

"But I'm not satisfied. The guys in the office talk to me and give me attention that I enjoy too much. I seem to be more important to them than I am to Ronnie. I'm afraid of what I'm feeling toward them. I need help; we need help. I'm sure Ronnie is completely unaware that we have a problem."

After Ronnie got over the initial shock that Julie felt so unwanted and neglected by him, his response was, "I can fix that. I can take her with me when I play golf if she'd be willing to go.

"Julie's right that we don't go places or do things," Ronnie continued. "I just don't think about things like that. I've been self-centered. It's so good to get home to peace and quiet—I work in a noisy factory—that I don't try to invent things to do. It used to be we didn't have money to eat out or take in movies and concerts, but finances are a bit more

56

stable now and we should take advantage of that. We used to play games like Scrabble. We just got out of the habit. I need her suggestions, though."

I find that most husbands are this agreeable, but, as a rule, they are not good at thinking up interesting things to do after work. If wives wait around for their husbands to work them into their schedules and suggest recreational ideas, they will end up like Julie—neglected.

Before they yield to someone else's attention, women have a responsibility to explain their need for prime-time activities with and attention from their husbands.

Contesting with Sports

While we are on this subject of importance, it is fitting that we mention the woes of sports' widows from husband-participation in summer league softball, fair weather golf, winter bowling, and TV spectator sports.

The only comfort I can offer is to admit that I, too, am a victim of TV sports. I advise women to learn the game, choose a favorite team, and take advantage of the commercial breaks.

Once while splashing around in the lonely self-pity pool, I complained to Jim about my slipping below football in importance to him. "Don't feel too badly, honey," he quipped, "I like you much better than basketball." Many wives solve their problem by reading or doing handwork while in their husbands' preoccupied presence.

Husbands do need to exercise discipline regarding time spent in pursuit of their own pleasures, whether it is a hobby, work, or sports, and be aware of their wives' need to rank first in importance—at least some of the time.

When a woman understands and appreciates her husband's instinctive need for financial security and his interest in things, being careful not to equate it with their being number-one in importance to him, communication which involves compromise will develop. And a husband, being aware of the wife's need to be assured in talk and in action that she is indeed number-one female in his life, will balance the act.

Just as the crankshaft powers the oil pump which lubricates all parts of the engine and is vital to a smooth-running engine, being number-one is the power a wife needs in a harmonious marriage relationship.

5

Applying Understanding

Henpecked Husband

Thelma Winters used a personal hurt to draw her husband into a revealing and healing conversation. During a heated disagreement over logistics of the family's schedule, Thelma's husband, Al, interjected, "The men at work are right when they say that I'm henpecked." Immediate painful shock registered in Thelma's face as his statement hit her. She had intentionally endeavored not to push her views on Al, especially since she had become a Christian and understood that selfishness and insecurity drive domineering women.

Her first impulse was to hide and cry. "How could this be?" she wondered. Thelma absolutely didn't want to be a domineering wife. She attempted to build up Al and to encourage him in his field where he was a success. And not only had she deemphasized her expertise at decision-making, but to encourage him to be more decisive she often went along with his opinions and direction although she silently disagreed.

For several years she had purposely played down her outgoing and confident personality so Al would not feel threatened by her, even to the point where friends and relatives noticed the change. She hated to fail, and evidently she had according to his coworkers.

Certainly, the men at work were wrong, but hearing that Al agreed with them not only hurt her immensely, but intimidated her from even defending herself.

Later that night she did shed some self-pitying tears. She wanted to discuss this subject, but didn't know how. Her heart was heavy, not knowing how to communicate.

"One of the discoveries of our time is that marriage is much better when people really are their true selves and really share their true feelings with each other," say David and Vera Mace in *Christian Freedom for Women*. "Much better, yes, but unfortunately, also much more difficult. The reason why most couples give up trying to be companions is that they just don't know how."

Because there definitely was a wedge developing between Thelma and Al, after receiving some encouragement from a friend she decided to risk another hurt and challenge the shop guys' opinion. So when she and Al were alone and had plenty of time to finish a conversation, she approached Al with the subject.

"Al, do you really agree with those fellows at work that you are henpecked?"

"I sure do!" he retorted with conviction, so unlike him because he generally avoided disagreements like the plague.

"I haven't been able to do the things I've wanted to for twelve years, ever since we've been married," he exploded.

Wow! What an accusation. Insult added to injury. Thelma's heart nearly broke, but she held back tears of defense that fought to be released and courageously continued.

"What would you like to do that you haven't been able to do because I didn't aprove or wouldn't let you?" Thelma inquired. "Name them for me."

Al contemplated for a while and then admitted slowly, "Actually, I guess the things I've really wanted to do, I've done, and the things I haven't done are because of lack of time or money—mostly money, and that's not your fault."

"Then, is the henpecking accusation based on the fact that I'm just more assertive and outspoken than you, rather than actually controlling your life?"

"That could be," he surmised, nodding his head.

"Then, down deep, are you just afraid of being henpecked?"

"I guess that's it," he agreed.

The conversation rolled spontaneously on into another delicate but important area they had never had courage to discuss before.

"Could it be, honey," Thelma speculated, "that since by nature I am more talkative and enthusiastic than you, that secretly you think I want to boss you around like your mother bossed your father?"

"Dad never got his way," Al said resolutely, "not unless he did things behind her back. There's no doubt that Mom controlled him and tried to change him," Al admitted.

"I'm sure you're aware that we aren't just like your mom and dad, Al," Thelma said. "You're quiet like your dad but you're willing to discuss differences. And being outgoing and confident is what your mother and I have in common, but that's about it. She was insecure and had to control everybody around her. But I don't need to be domineering to be happy. Do you agree?"

"I never really thought about it before, Thelma," Al said. "But I do see that we're different people. You don't seem to be afraid of anything or anybody."

"Could this be why you are reluctant to encourage and praise me for things I do? Are you afraid that I will become overbearing?"

"I didn't ever think you needed encouragement or praise, to be truthful, Thelma. You already do things well and seem to keep yourself up without my help. I'm the one who needs encouragement and prodding."

This was Thelma's golden opportunity to inform Al how much she had longed for and needed his approval and his encouragement. She assured him that she had no intention or desire to control him nor to dictate to him what he could or could not do.

"I just hunger for better communication and opportunity to work together on some things," Thelma said.

This in-depth conversation not only destroyed Al's crippling misconception but opened his eyes to Thelma's honest intentions, exposing her need for his appreciation.

Many men are like Al, afraid that wives will take advantage of their good nature and compliments just to steal second base, so they withhold any form of appreciation.

Al and Thelma's relationship has improved because they risked discussing feelings and attitudes. A person cannot appreciate another's position and opinions until he or she truly understands. But understanding does not come without open, honest dialogue.

Conversation is an art. The dos and don'ts of conversation—the magic of using "I" statements rather than "you" statements; the wisdom of ridding vocabulary of destructive sarcasms; dealing with single issues; and choosing the right time—are discussed in detail in my book *Encouragement: A Wife's Special Gift*. You will also find these effective conversation methods sprinkled throughout the rest of this book.

The importance of open and honest discussion, without fear, within a marriage is similar to the necessity of maintaining ample, clean oil in the crankcase of an engine if it is to function smoothly.

6

Awarding Approval

Women have such an appetite for approval that they will go to extremes to get it, suffering disappointment when anticipated support does not materialize, fizzles, or ends abruptly. They are often overwhelmed with guilt feelings, stemming from any negative or inferior source.

Receiving Recognition

When I was twenty-five and had several children, I felt like running away. We lived on rattlesnake hill in far west Texas where neighbors were few and far away. Jim managed a gas business and pastored a mission church as well. I felt like a robot, taking service calls for him, fixing meals for his unpredictable arrival time, and serving as unofficial assistant pastor.

Jim was often so tired after a twelve-hour work

day, that he had little energy to contribute to my emotional needs. Although I was busy all day doing the things I enjoyed—sewing, studying, teaching the children, visiting for the church, cleaning, baking, and so on, I was still not satisfied.

I was so hungry for adult conversation and Jim's approval that I would follow him into the bathroom, pelting him with one question after the other. I would ask him, "Did you think about me today?" to which he would often reply with regrettable honesty, "No, I didn't. I had too many other things on my mind." Then, I would cry.

I didn't know it then, but realized it later that all I needed to hear was, "Ruthie, I appreciate how hard you have worked today," or "My, it's good to be with you," or "I appreciate your taking the business calls and making the visits to the church people."

Fortunately, Jim is a very fast learner and I keep little to myself. So we discovered each other's verbal needs. Our communication has been on good footing ever since we learned to understand each other's preferences and appreciate each other's needs.

In turn, then, I shower on him those things he needs to hear and do for him those things which he revels in having done for him. We are busy helping each other become the best person each can become, helping each other reach personal goals. To me, that's an ideal setup. This does not mean that we never disagree or suffer disappointment, but we have learned the value of talking and listening.

Bestowing Attention

Husbands' public pride in their wives satisfies women's craving for belonging. Most women concede that they like to be seen with their husbands in public so people will know this handsome, important man loves me, is proud to be with me, and chose me for his companion.

Many women also enjoy their mate giving a little public expression of affection and recognition so that others will know that he really does adore and approve of his spouse.

Women delight to hear from their husbands, "I enjoy being with you," "You are a lovely person," "I like the natural way you have of making others feel important," "You're pretty," and similar uplifting statements.

An old proverb says, "The reason average woman would rather have beauty than brains is because she knows the average man can see better than he can think."

Though the majority of women are not blessed with gorgeous figures, beautiful voices, and pretty faces, pleasant and caring personalities can characterize any woman who is willing to pay the price and cultivate it.

Flaunting Attention

Wives love to brag to other women, "My husband cleans the bathroom," "scrubs the kitchen floor," "brings me breakfast in bed," "carries out the garbage," "helps me clean house," and so on. It is

not that the women want their husbands to be their servants, but that they need reassurance of their personal worth.

I feel important and appreciated when I go in to bed and see that Jim, very conscious of my dislike of getting into a cold bed, has already turned on the electric blanket. It is a little thing, but is important.

Dissatisfied women, those who are not receiving enough or the right kind of attention, often engage in the sad game of husband comparison. One lady wanted to shape her husband into a little of Ellen's husband who does dishes; Fran's husband, who diapers the baby; Edna's husband, who brings gifts and gives special attention; and Myra's father, who fixes everything. "Yes, this will make you a great husband," she reasons silently. "Then, I'll be happy," she thinks. Even when a woman is successful in forcing her spouse into a composite of all these attributes, she ultimately winds up with someone else besides the man she chose, and much to her disillusionment.

Some husbands are reluctant to give their wives recognition, praise, and attention for fear such actions might indicate a yielding to presumed female desires to control their husbands.

So women must learn how to interpret their attention needs to their husbands in a nonthreatening way if they want their approval. I'll indulge in another personal tale to illustrate the kind of risk that is involved in interpreting one's needs.

Innocent Oversight

Eleven months after we were married, anticipation mounted as my first birthday as Ruth Ward approached. The day was about to end without one sign that Jim was aware it was my special day. Birthday celebrations in my family were always a big deal—decorated and candled cakes magically appeared and wrapped gifts were always creatively camouflaged until just the right moment.

Jim had indeed forgotten my birthday—an unforgiveable oversight. I was crushed. As usual, I about drowned in bitter tears of self-pity. Being thirteen hundred miles from home intensified my disappointment and feeling of neglect.

Jim took me into his arms, dried my tears, and inquired tenderly, "Honey, what had you wanted me to do?" It never dawned on me that birthdays in his family were no big deal. How did he know what I expected? So I told him what I had anticipated, risking that he would reject my admitted need for attention as immature and childish.

The risk was worth it! He has not missed my birthday since. In fact, I have had a delicious, homemade cake every year and a gift—even when he has been out of town—for the more than twenty-five years that we have been married. I will admit that I reminded him the second year that a special day was nearing.

Jim has gotten some mileage out of the experience, too, taking great delight in sharing it in premarital counseling sessions to caution naive bridegrooms.

Some women are embarrassed to admit that they want to be remembered on special days like Mother's Day and Valentine's Day. They believe that telling a husband they want a gift smacks of self-centeredness and pride. So they say nothing, choosing to battle hurt as these special times of the year roll around unobserved.

Ladies, don't keep your desires to yourself. You not only hurt yourself, but deny your husband the privilege of giving you the attention that will build his ego as he meets your needs.

Mothers appreciate fathers encouraging and assisting their children in remembering special days, too. This is a great way to get sons ready to be attentive husbands.

Naturally, attention and gift giving is a two-way street, but usually females need little encouragement to bestow this kind of attention on men.

Understanding Sexual Attention

Wives who watch soap operas' glamorous excitement invite discontentment when they compare the physical attention they get from their spouses with the fantasy world.

The freedom, excitement, and glamour presented on TV as well as in movies make some marriages seem bland by comparison. Some wives, who crave action, are unhappy until some type of conflict is an actuality in their own marriage. Many women enjoy knowing their husband is jealous and even provoke it because they are so eager for their mate's approval and acceptance.

In desperation, many women resort to using sexual privilege as a control lever. This is unfair to both husband and wife. My book *Encouragement: A Wife's Special Gift* discusses in detail the importance and place of sexual relationship, so I will not elaborate here, except for a few remarks regarding some current dangerous concepts.

Some women assume wrongly that sex attention proves that love is alive and active. Unfortunately, many psychologists and marriage counselors suggest that a good sexual relationship is the most important dimension of a marriage. They even go so far as to call sex the cement that holds marriage together.

If sex is the cement that holds marriages together, it would be forever broken since sexual fulfillment for the woman is a result or outgrowth of a trust relationship which is dependent on good communication about finances, values, and respect. In most cases, when conflicts arise, the woman's interest in sex generally wanes accordingly, though her love for her spouse does not diminish.

The astounding fact that many spouses continue engaging in sex with their partner while estranged and subsequently proceed with divorce proves that sex, itself, will not hold a marriage together. Sex is more like a fragrance exuding from mutual trust and respect borne out of careful understanding and applied appreciation.

Normal women are eager to engage in satisfying sexual relationships with their husbands when they receive quality daily affection and attention. Immature husbands who don't understand the con-

74

nection between sex and respect, often look outside the marriage for sexual satisfaction at the expense of their wives' self-esteem.

Dr. James Dobson, Sr., says in *Family Under Fire* (Beacon Hill Press, 1976) that since men tend to meet their own needs for self-esteem through their work, they find it easy to neglect giving the necessary attention to their wives. In the next few pages we will see how subtly this can happen.

Falling out of Acquaintance

George and Jenny Lane, both Christians in an evangelical denomination, and involved in church activities, have been married seventeen years. Marrying right out of high school, Jenny sacrificially encouraged George through college, like many wives do, and on to a managerial position. She has taken great pride in her personal beauty as well as in maintaining a lovely home, and in lavishing exceptional care on her husband and children.

The fact that her self-confidence and personal happiness rested totally on George and the children never concerned Jenny, until George became fascinated with an assertive and confident coworker.

Spurned by the excitement of secrecy and the challenge of the little boy desire of what an affair with another woman would be like to a guy who had never dated anyone besides Jenny, George—the last person in the world anyone would suspect—fell victim to a brief affair.

Jenny was devastated. Where had she failed? Her idealistic castle crumbled. "All I ever wanted was to be a dedicated Christian mother and wife. In exchange, I wanted an attentive, hardworking, confident husband. I thought our marriage was perfect," she wept.

What had happened? A very common occurrence in Christian homes today—a marriage friendship existed instead of a marriage companionship. Whose fault? Mostly Jenny's. Here's why.

Because Jenny lacked confidence and felt educationally inferior to George, all through the years she had willingly accepted the blame for problems, ignoring her own personal dissatisfaction with their lack of conversation and companionship. She had kept disagreements to herself. She had placed George on such a high pedestal that she was afraid to infringe on his time to interpret her hungers for his attention, a hunger that had grown as the children entered junior high and became more independent, not needing her so much.

Jenny never wanted to be a nagging wife like her mother was nor ever wanted to provoke an argument. She was after a perfect marriage, and somewhere she had learned that the absence of argument insured this. She also prided herself in that she never refused George's sexual needs.

Because she kept all these feelings to herself, George naturally was unaware of her need for his support and was also blind to his own selfish immaturities. Since he received the bulk of his self-esteem from his work and assumed that Jenny gleaned her quota from homemaking responsibilities, Jenny's naivete and negligence fashioned George into an insensitive husband. This pattern was killing their marriage. They were falling out of acquaintance like a battery running out of juice.

In a growing marriage the wife does not endure injustices and deny emotional hunger for support, but rather takes pains to cultivate good communication, which demands the airing of differing opinions, admitting disappointments, and risking disagreements. Peacemaking is not silent acceptance of another's preferences, but facing obstacles of anger squarely and discussing hurt feelings and misunderstandings. This leads to respect and companionship.

George had learned to regard Jenny as his personal maid and mistress. Though he loved her, he searched elsewhere for a challenging companionship with someone who stood up to him as an individual and admitted needs that he could fill.

George could not fulfill the physical needs of two women without getting into all kinds of difficulty. George lost his job and he and his family moved to another state where he found a new position. Through counseling, Jenny and George discovered their unmet needs and the advantage that conversation contributes to a full understanding.

Jenny entered college and is developing confidence as well as interests outside her husband and home. Jenny needed help to discover her own needs before she could interpret her deep feelings and needs to George.

"Please share my story," Jenny urged. "I would be happy to talk with any woman who is going through what I did. We are proof that people can rebuild a relationship. I thank God for leading me to get help and I give Him glory for giving me patience to understand myself and George. Our home can once again honor Him."

Just as the transmission in an automobile requires plenty of transmission fluid—a type of oil—before it can dispatch power from the engine to the driving axle, so women rely on attention and approval from their husbands to transmit self-esteem.

If one of the cooling lines in the transmission mechanism develops a leak, the level of fluid gets too low, and the car will stop. Similarly, because George was unaware of the importance of his contribution of attention to Jenny, the appreciation level dropped, and their marriage relationship stopped.

7

Gifting with Praise

Wives function on appreciation. In fact, a wife will ordinarily put up with any inconvenience or deprivation if she knows her husband sincerely appreciates her contribution and/or sacrifice.

But many wives are reluctant to express their needs to their husbands because they are afraid of two things—that their husbands will not care or understand, and that praise will not be spontaneous.

So women imagine what they want to hear or have done and when they do not hear it or experience it, they are hurt.

David and Vera Mace in *Christian Freedom for Women* say: "The average husband is ham-handed and helpless when he is confronted by his wife's real emotions. So she learns to bottle them, and he learns not to ask her about her deeper thoughts and feelings and not to tell her about his. Since their attempts to achieve intimacy produce alarming results, they back up and settle for a superficial relationship which is not really satisfying and is not really what they wanted. They become disillusioned and drift apart. This is a pretty good description of how millions of American marriages get onto the rocks."

To illustrate this facet of appreciation, I'll relate another personal experience.

Hungering for Praise

Years ago, I went to a great deal of trouble to prepare a sumptuous cookbook dinner to convey to Jim how much his bride of one month loved him. The longer I slaved, the more my female appetite was whetted for the reciprocal praise I expected.

The atmosphere was electric and my heart was bursting with pride as I set before him on the candle-lit table my savory and beautiful creation—quite an accomplishment for a new cook, I thought.

I waited breathlessly as without comment, Jim took the first bite. But the words of praise my ears and heart were geared to hear did not come. Instead, he asked politely, "What is it?"

"Stuffed cabbage rolls," I said guardedly. "Do you like them?" I asked, a lump of disappointment already forming in my throat.

"Why didn't you just boil the cabbage?" he asked softly. "That's the way I like it." Needless to say, my eyes brimmed with hot tears.

"But it took the entire day to fix this," I argued. "Besides, I'm exhausted," I sobbed. "I did it all for you."

This could have ended with my leaving the table with hurt feelings, pledging in my heart never again to waste time trying to please this ungrateful man. Fortunately, it ended better than that.

"Honey," Jim consoled, "I like plain food. If you want to please me, just keep it simple. I don't want you to wear yourself out cooking elaborate meals for me," he comforted. "I love you for who you are and not for how hard you work to please me."

I didn't get my supply of verbal praise that day, but it provided an opportunity to learn volumes about communication and rightly relating to each other.

Jim learned, also, that since women instinctively go to extra trouble to please in order to receive praise, husbands should give them praise for their effort and the thought behind it whether or not it is their favorite dish.

I learned that when I want to be assured of getting spontaneous praise for something I cook, it is smarter to fix corn bread and beans or boiled cabbage, rather than an exotic dish that merely demonstrates my culinary skills.

This incident illustrates not only one type of appreciation a woman needs from her husband but how open and honest communication can transform lack of understanding, disappointment, and hurt feelings into a valuable learning experience, equipping a husband and wife to be knowledgeable and sensitive to one another's needs.

Appreciation is something like the oil that is added regularly to an engine. When the oil level gets low, it is time to add more. Wives who know

when they need a dose of praise, should also know where the oil can is.

Understanding Praise

Wives need to get acquainted with their husband's style and/or negligence of complimenting. Since husbands tend to mimic their dads, a good place to begin is to study your husband's father. If he heard his father say, "good meal," "the house looks nice," "I like your outfit," "I'm impressed with the way you handled that," and so on, chances are that he will automatically gift you with the same kind of praise.

Fishing for compliments to satisfy a hunger for recognition does not satisfy. "If you have to beg for a compliment," one wife declared, "what good is it?"

Most people are uncomfortable when someone really pours the compliments on, like, "You are a wonderful person," "You are beautiful," "You do things so well," preferring rather that their activity or action be noticed rather than their character. Haim Ginott explains this concept well in *Between Parent and Child* (Avon Books, 1965). "Direct praise of personality, like direct sunlight, is uncomfortable and blinding. It is embarrassing for a person to be told that he is wonderful, angelic, generous, and humble. He feels called on to deny at least part of the praise." Ginott goes on to say that praise should deal with efforts and achievements.

When a wife is receiving her quota of praise, she will not need to bait her husband or others for compliments.

Pleasing for Praise

Women smile with relief when they discover that other women struggle with the same problems and motivations. For instance, dozens of women have admitted that they plow through a messy house, prepare delicious meals, and so on for the same main reason—their husband's approval. "Let's straighten the house before Daddy comes home," a mother instructs.

Everything I did was for Jim—every floor I scrubbed, meal I prepared, and pie I baked. I wanted him to appreciate what a good wife I was and to know how much I loved him. But Jim did not realize that at first. When he did discover my motive he did not want to be the blame for how tired presenting a spotless house made me. And expressing approval about the condition of the house was not one of his natural talents. When ten or fifteen minutes had passed after Jim's arrival home from work, and he had not said anything, my disappointment would surface.

"What's wrong?" he would ask.

"Didn't you notice the kitchen floor? I waxed it today. I also washed and starched the bathroom curtains."

"It always looks nice, Ruthie," he would say.

"But I did it for you," I would reason. That always blew his mind.

"Well, don't work so hard, then, if you do it for me," he would scold. "I don't demand that." Jim was a good teacher.

I have relaxed a lot in my personal slave-driving

efforts as my security and trust in Jim has grown. But one of the hardest things for me yet is to get excited about preparing a big meal if Jim won't be there. That's a compliment to him.

What has happened in many marriages is that the wife who goes to work for financial or boredom reasons receives praise and appreciation from coworkers that she has not been receiving from her husband. When the appreciation level at work exceeds that at home, the woman begins to evaluate what means the most—financial security or self-esteem. This simple conflict is tearing marriages apart. Some examples follow.

Pleasing for Thanks

Jennifer Cline, who went to work to help meet the family budget, found herself bogged down with housework, child care, and chauffeuring children.

Although she did a little moaning about her extra heavy load, Ralph did not take hints quickly and continued to let her pick up after him and expected things to go on as usual.

One evening, in the midst of all these pressures, when it was obvious he was not going to gift her with the words of praise that she so longed to hear, Jennifer could hold the tears of resentment no longer. "Couldn't you even say thank you to me?" she pleaded. "Not today," he said curtly. "This has been a bad day for me; I have no thank yous to give."

Her heart was further broken because Ralph didn't even ask how her day had been. All Ralph would have to do to make Jennifer's sacrifice worthwhile would be to hug her, hold her, and say, "I appreciate you, darling. I am a lucky man." With those words of encouragement, she would not be able to do enough.

Organizing for Praise

A high school teacher and mother of several small children shared her experiences during an especially busy week. As a church committee chairperson, she had to really manage her time so as not to upset the regular routine of the household. Her husband assisted her without complaint.

Though she was pleased with how every detail dove-tailed, by the end of the week, she thought, "How nice it would be to be a husband and just follow someone's well thought-out plans and merely follow instructions. The longer she thought about it, the angrier she became that she was working so hard to manage phone calls, child and home care, hot meals, clean clothes, correcting school papers, and preparing lunches. And her husband just seemed to take it for granted. He did not marvel at this at all. It did not bother her so much that he did not help, but rather that he did not seem to notice that all this coordination required astute planning, delegating of responsibilities, and discipline on her part. She finally said, "Rex, haven't you noticed that things have gone very smoothly this week and you and the kids haven't suffered a bit because of the extra running and phone calls I've had to handle. Don't you appreciate it?"

"Yeah," he answered bewilderedly. "Thanks. I didn't know you needed that."

"It's not the same," she said, "when I have to solicit thanks. Evidently, I just felt used by my own design. But it encourages me to keep things stress-free when I hear you say it first."

Praise is encouragement to work a little harder, bake another cake, visit again, appreciate yourself.

Receiving regular praise is as essential for a woman's self-esteem, and thus a smooth-running marriage, as adequate lubrication of the engine is required for an automobile's trouble-free operation.

8

Recognizing Individuality

Homemaking Blahs

"I hate housework," Stephanie blurted out after Stan mentioned that a colony of spiders had taken up residency in the spare bedroom.

"If those spiders bother you so much," she challenged, "you know where the broom and dustpan are."

"Housework is not a man's job," he yelled.

Wow! This dialogue will lead no where except to clenched fists and tears.

Most women find housework exasperating, boring, and a necessary evil. "It is never finished and rarely appreciated," Stephanie droned. "I don't know how my mom stood it all those years. One thing is sure, I'm more like my dad."

Men have a tendency—and so do many women—

to believe that wives and/or mothers, naturally take great delight in washing windows, scrubbing floors, wiping fingerprints from woodwork, cleaning ovens, straightening drawers, shining silver, dusting baseboards and furniture, vacuuming rugs, emptying trash cans, shampooing rugs, washing piles of laundry, mending rips and replacing buttons, sweeping cobwebby basements and dusty garages, scouring pans, and so on. Some of us really do enjoy this labor of love. The majority, however, do home chores because someone has to do them and traditionally it falls into the woman's arms because she is generally the last one to be employed outside the home.

"She has the time," I have heard husbands rationalize, "so, it's her job." The traditional idea that homemaking fulfills every woman is ruining marriage. As David and Vera Mace say in *Christian Freedom for Women,* "At the heart of most broken marriages today lies the fact that people know what is companionship marriage; but they can't make this work because they have been trained for traditional marriage. It's as if we trained an athlete carefully for the hundred-yard dash, and then he found himself entered for the high jump."

How it comforts and encourages women to learn that it is normal and okay for a female to dislike housework. It boggles the minds of many traditionalists to hear of men assuming household chores because they really enjoy doing them.

For other men, however, until they spend some time at home all day taking care of the myriad details that have to be done over and over plus taking care of young children, they cannot possibly appreciate the significance of homemaking blahs. If husbands would dare to challenge wives to exchange lifestyles, many women would jump at the chance.

One of my favorite family stories dates back to college days when I consented to use my secretarial skills two days a week to help with finances. Jim scheduled his classes on the other three days. His plan was to study while he cared for our three preschoolers, ages six months, two, and three and a half.

Although I am one of those wives and mothers who loves housework (even cleaning the oven and washing windows on the outside), working in an office for two days a week was a refreshing break for me. But staying at home was not so nice for Jim.

I'll never forget one midmorning call home. Things had evidently not gone well for Jim because when I asked, "What are you planning to fix for lunch?" he replied with a frustrated sigh, "I think we'll have fried David legs."

Those six months as mother-figure taught Jim more wife and mother appreciation than all my explaining and complaining ever could have. In fact, that experience has supplied him with enough understanding to last our entire marriage with extra to bubble over onto young mothers in our congregations. He is very aware of their draining lifestyle.

Stephanie had to force herself to take care of cleaning details because she was afraid someone would accuse her of not being a good wife. Though she loved to entertain, the main reason she resisted inviting company was that she knew Steve was embarrassed if the windows weren't sparkling and if one could write his name on the dusty coffee table.

Housework seemed noncreative to Stephanie compared with work involving people. She wanted to renew the real estate license she earned before the children were born, adding to her Bible studies, PTA, and being a room mother at school.

Some husbands feel threatened when wives want gainful employment, particularly if the wife's earning power is greater. In that case, the husband's ego often takes a plunge.

Stephanie explained to Steve that she would be happier to use her time cooking balanced meals, spending creative and quality time with him and the children, working in the yard and garden, and dabbling in real estate a couple evenings every week. She just could not take care of all the inside cleaning, too, and still have time to involve herself in the things she really enjoyed.

After this conversation, Steve suggested setting aside a little money for hired help with the housework to release Stephanie to engage without hassle in satisfying activities. Knowing that Steve was willing to care for the children two evenings a week while she showed houses lifted her spirits considerably.

Steve even decided, since he was the one who particularly appreciated sparkling windows and spiderless corners, that rather than pay someone else to do that work, he would not mind assuming that responsibility. No more did Stephanie have to feel guilty about her individual preferences or the fact that Steve helped with inside—female—chores.

I have heard women sigh as they hear their friends share how their husbands scrub and wax the floors, wash windows, clean the oven, and cook. One husband I know will not allow anyone else in the family to load the dishwasher, claiming to be the expert. Switching and sharing jobs is not a sin. I know a minister who takes care of all the laundry, including the ironing; an Air Force pilot who scrubs floors; and an automobile salesman who cooks all the meals and does the baking.

If a woman prefers to mow grass, tinker with the car, remodel the house, or build furniture—traditionally male jobs—husbands should allow them the privilege of doing what they enjoy.

If a woman prefers to teach school; work in a factory, bank, or office; serve as a nurse or as a clerk in a department store, and to hire someone to do some or all of her housework, that should be her prerogative.

We all have to do many things we do not enjoy, but our lives do not have to be a steady diet of duties that not only turn us off but usurp all our time.

Developing Individuality

Because children's mommy needs decrease each year, empty nest syndrome—boredom—eventually creeps up on mom and pushes her out the door.

This happens sooner than it used to because

parents are having fewer children. By age forty a woman finds her children starting to leave home.

Sonja Griffin wrestled with this problem. Here's how she described what she felt.

"It suddenly dawned on me that I had achieved everything I had set out to do. Travel, be an airline stewardess, get married, live in a farmhouse on the outskirts of a big city, and have children. That's all happened. I'm only forty. In a few years my kids will all be gone. They don't need me through the day now. I'm scared. What shall I do? I'm not skilled in anything. If I have time on my hands at this point, what will it be like in five years?

"My husband Ken doesn't understand that I'm going through some phase. He thinks I have enough to do with keeping the house, cooking, waiting for the kids to come home from school, attending PTA programs, and keeping busy in the church. He just can't look ahead.

"I've tried to convince him for two years that I'm bored. He finally understands that I need something more than what I have. He is sure I'm just going through the change in life. But, anyway, this fall I began college. I'm so excited. I feel like a brand new person. I have suffered from guilt feelings mixed with delight."

Ken's ability to appreciate Sonja's need to grow and his encouragement for her to develop will boomerang, promising him a happier wife and better communication. Consequently, a satisfying and more exciting marriage will emerge.

Just as a drop or two of oil deftly applied to a

door hinge silences squeaks, so sensitive husbands are in a unique position to help their wives find fulfillment by encouraging them to recognize and pursue their individual preferences and ease out of the homemaking blahs.

9

Lending Assistance

Whose House Is It, Anyway?

"I quit being the maid," Janeen Sanders declared during a marriage counseling session. "My blood just boils when clothes I've pressed are tried on once and tossed on the floor and the house I've straightened a dozen times is blazing with trails of books, papers, shoes, snack dishes, apple cores—you name it. Nobody cares. I'm just fed up!" Tears of self-pity welled up in Janeen's eyes. "So, I fixed them. I went on strike last week—resigned. Didn't cook, clean, wash, vacuum. Didn't lose any pay, either," she added sarcastically.

"What did you think about all that, Pete?" I inquired cautiously, hoping to ease the atmosphere a little.

"It shocked us," he said, nodding his head. "The

kids were angry with her. I guess I was, too, but she does have a problem. She gets no cooperation. Everyone is so involved in school, church, and with friends that it seems no one has time to help. I do feel sorry for Janeen. I wish she didn't have to work," he added sympathetically.

"That's not the point!" Janeen raged, sitting up very straight. "I'm glad I have to work. I love my job because taking complete care of a house all day, everyday, bores me to death—nothing but empty routine. But I feel keeping the house tidy is not just my problem, but our problem.

"The kids are all healthy teenagers, and if I continue to be their personal maid, how and when are they going to learn self-respect and discipline? I have to have support from Pete and cooperation from everyone, including him. After all, whose house is it, anyway? It's not just mine."

Janeen voices hundreds of mothers' cries. Some of these frustrated mothers vent their anger by actually leaving home, which Janeen was on the verge of doing. She, and millions like her, need emotional hospitality.

"I work all day," Janeen explained, "then I rush home to prepare supper, clean up left-over breakfast mess, throw a load of clothes in the washer, and discover to my dismay that the last load of clothes lies in a wrinkled pile in the dryer. As I hurry out the door to chauffeur Betsy to piano lessons, I catch a glimpse of the streaked bay window that hasn't been cleaned for two months and am filled with guilt. Where does it stop? No one does anything unless I ask. Then, when he does it, it's done as a favor to me."

Even though many women dislike housework, a great part of their self-respect is tied to the way the home looks. "If mothers would stay home like they are supposed to," some insensitive people chide, "these problems would disappear."

The person who makes a statement like this often comes from the over-fifty generation or from a family where a second check is not a necessity or where the wife does not want to work. Unfortunately, many women today have no choice about outside employment.

Some husbands with the misconception that females were created primarily to make men's lives easier and to wait on children are often cynical about their wive's emotional need to work and their pleas for household assistance as well. The men who threaten, "If she wants to work, she has to pay the price for that privilege of freedom" need help in understanding that this attitude is demeaning as well as nonbiblical.

Smaller families, push-button appliances, processed food, nursery schools, and many other things leave intelligent young women looking for ways to deal creatively and practically with valuable free time and great potential.

"The plain truth is that running a household was once an art, and is no longer so. . . . We must face the fact that the rewards of homemaking have greatly diminished," say David and Vera Mace, in *Christian Freedom for Women.*

Whether women choose employment outside

the home because they have to or to keep skills alive, to provide college savings, or to give themselves a mental challenge, adjustment inside the home is mandatory.

Husband, children, and those women who try to be supermoms need to acknowledge that it is impossible and unrealistic to add full- or part-time employment and continue the former quality full-time homemaking responsibilities.

Even when a mother is unemployed, a large portion of her week can be overloaded with running forgotten items to school, marketing, visiting or corresponding with relatives, doing church or volunteer work, cleaning, cooking, washing, and so on. All mothers instinctively hunger for appreciation and cooperation from husband and children—the objects of their endeavors. Mothers resent being merely regarded as machines. Moving from being taken for granted to being respected requires family growth.

Paul, in writing to the New Testament believers, challenged them to work for unity in their church family. We, too, must strive for this same unity in our diversified American lives.

Along with harmony, Ephesians 6:1 commands children to obey their parents. How can these spiritual concepts become a reality in a modern American home?

Here's what happened in the Sanders's home. Janeen listed all the jobs that needed to be done daily with the approximate time each required. Her list looked like this:

Vacuum living and dining room—15 minutes
Sweep and mop kitchen—10 minutes
Feed cat—5 minutes
Scrub pans—20 minutes
Wash clothes—10 minutes
Empty dryer—10 minutes
Set table—10 minutes
Empty dishwasher—15 minutes
Cook dinner—30 minutes
Carry out trash—5 minutes
Clean bathroom—10 minutes

After praying together about it, Pete and Janeen called a family meeting. Pete explained to the three apprehensive teenagers that with mother's new working schedule, she was no longer able to assume total care of the home nor could she cope with a messy house.

"Your mother has listed daily duties with the approximate time each takes. Each of us will make our choice of thirty minutes' worth of jobs—one big one or a couple of little ones. Besides these jobs," he continued, "each person will be responsible for picking up all his or her trails and keeping his or her bedroom presentable."

When Pete also chose jobs, the children were encouraged to fall in line and cooperate. "Let's give this a week's try," he said, "and if you want to switch jobs after that, we will."

The next week, Janeen was jubilant. "I have really had a wonderful week," she glowed. "The kids have been just wonderful and so has Pete. You wouldn't believe how sweet the atmosphere is now. I haven't had to scream at the kids once.

"For the first time in months," Janeen sighed, "I have time to read the Bible and pray before going to the office because Betsy sets the table, Ted empties the dishwasher, and Jonathan feeds the cat. And, Betsy, bless her heart, has even elected to pack my lunch. I still do the cooking. No one volunteered for that job."

"What are your observations, Pete?" I asked.

"I'm learning much and have changed a lot, too," he said. "You're looking at the best bathroom cleaner in this county!" he boasted. "I didn't realize how many trails I was leaving behind until I started throwing my own clothes in the hamper and picking up shoes and papers. It just takes a minute for me to make the bed, too. No wonder Janeen was discouraged. We have really made headway in the last week in our marriage relationship," Pete said, as he lovingly squeezed Janeen's hand.

"A tender side effect of all this," Janeen shared with a tear in her eye, "is last night I found a note on my pillow which read, 'Dear Mom, Thanks for putting up with me. We've all been so selfish. I love you. Betsy.'"

Open and honest communication in marriage and family is not easy, but with a little bit of help, it can be cultivated as in the Sanders's experience.

After a couple months of experimenting, the Sanders found it necessary to have another family meeting to make some adjustments, but their glowing reports indicate that this plan is certainly workable.

The husband should be the first to recognize his

wife's needs and see that she receives support and assistance.

Just as every five thousand miles or so, contaminated oil needs to be completely drained out and fresh oil put in in order to prevent premature failure of the engine, so appreciating mom and sharing the work load—whether she works outside the home or not—not only gives her a new lease on life but also forestalls discouragement, known as "burnout," to say nothing of the excellent training children receive in caring and cooperating.

10

Encouraging Respect

Jan and Carlton Johnson were at each other's throats about everything. They could not agree about finances, recreation, disciplining children, or even on menus.

Carlton was very organized. Jan was more casual. She washed laundry when she got ready and not at the beginning of each day as Carlton suggested. He griped about her not taking his shirts out of the dryer immediately. Though he admitted she would press them, she did not do it on his time schedule.

He also disapproved of her emptying the dishwasher as she set the table for the next meal rather than as soon as it was finished washing. "Why can't she be more organized?" he asked.

He was hurt that Jan chose to sleep late except on days she had to go to work. His idea was that good wives rise early, don a starched apron and bright disposition and prepare breakfast. She did not even like to eat breakfast.

When she did make an attempt to please him by dragging herself up to prepare his breakfast, he commented about her solemnity. "I admit I am not what you'd call bubbly," Jan agreed, "but I resent him calling me 'grumpy.'"

Carlton and Jan were different in many ways. One thing was certain, they could not hold a conversation without it ending in putdowns and accusations, slammed doors, and streams of tears. So they did not talk.

Because Jan did not meet Carlton's expectations on all these matters of organization, his approval of her was nil. He demonstrated displeasure by picking at everything she did and did not do, thinking she would finally learn how to be a decent housewife.

The more Carlton criticized, the more defensive and stubborn Jan became. Although Jan was acutely aware that her husband was not happy with her, she did not know how to alter his opinions without changing her own personality. She was just as unhappy about his finicky ways, though she withheld criticism.

Things had reached the dangerous stage because Jan was not crying anymore. She simply did not care. "I'm tired of his guilt trips," she stated firmly. Jan wanted out of the marriage. That is what brought them for help.

Our view of ourselves bounces off what others say and how they respond to what we do. Jan was receiving too many negative bounce-backs. Carlton was killing Jan's spirit.

The Johnsons' relationship at this point resembled what happens to wheel bearings when the grease runs dry. They squeal until finally they burn out, bringing the automobile to a screeching halt.

The Mechanics of Conversation

Before communication happens, couples must understand and appreciate the other's unique characteristics, then accept each other as he or she is. In the process of dialogue, the Johnsons not only discovered revealing things about themselves, but also got a handle on the mechanics of conversation as well. Here is a sample of how that conversation progressed.

"One gripe I have," Carlton shared, "is that Jan never shuts the kitchen cabinet doors. She is so sloppy. It just takes a second to close them. I've asked her over and over to please shut them. I just can't stand to eat a meal with eleven doors wide open."

"It's my turn," Jan declared. "First of all, I don't leave all the doors open all the time. Second, I don't think he understands what a drag it is to open and close those stupid doors all the time. He threatened to put locks on them," Jan sneared. "I don't think he has any right to talk to me like I'm a child. I resent that! Furthermore, I can't see anything wrong with doors being open while I'm working. My shelves don't look that bad. It is just a lot of trouble to close them every time I get something out. It's my kitchen. I don't see why it is any of his business how I choose to keep it. I don't bother his workshop and tools."

After much discussion about other related likes and dislikes, we returned to the cabinet doors' affair which revealed the basic problem of mutual lack of respect.

Carlton verbalized disappointment that Jan was not organized and neat. Unfortunately, he thought that pointing out all of her shortcomings (in his opinion) and failures would encourage her to become neat and disciplined like he was. He could not have been more wrong. He accused her of even becoming worse on purpose. She admitted that the more he complained, the less she felt like pleasing him and the messier she got. Neither wanted to budge an inch. Jan wanted Carlton's approval and praise, which is an outgrowth of respect. Carlton wanted her to care enough about him to keep the house as he wanted it. They had reached a dead end.

In finer analysis, we discovered that the gaping cabinets actually violated Carlton's natural bent to orderliness, making him feel insecure and untidy. When Jan learned that the open cabinets had more to do with him than with her, she was quite willing to try harder to keep them closed. So they compromised. She promised to close the doors, and he promised not to be critical of her home lifestyle.

During the next visit, Carlton was delighted to share that the problem with the cabinet doors was indeed solved, that Jan had bent over backwards to keep them shut. And he sincerely appreciated her effort. Likewise, with smiles, Jan reported that Carlton had kept criticism to a minimum. They had had a good week.

"I just realized something while sitting here," Jan surmised. "Even though I closed the cupboards all week, I still resented having to do it. Now I know why I prefer to leave them ajar. They bang! And I hate noise."

She revealed something about herself that neither she nor Carlton had understood and appreciated.

"Well, I can fix that," Carlton crowed. "I'll put magnets on them to cut down on the noise."

"It's a deal!" Jan nodded. "Then I'll be doubly glad to close them."

A picky little problem was solved, but not without miles of conversation. In the process of exchanging true feelings, Carlton and Jan gathered up deeper understanding and new appreciation for each other. Carlton was unaware that he had a certain prescribed mold set for Jan. Now, he was willing to let her be herself and decide her own schedule. Had their relationship continued with him unhappy and judgmental about the way she chose to handle her chores and her reacting defensively, their marriage certainly would have painfully and unnecessarily ended.

Just as some dismantling is necessary before wheel bearings can be repacked, so engaging in open conversation where likes and dislikes are freely shared must precede a healthy mutual respect.

11

Acknowledging Equality

Innocent Inequity

While out walking one fall morning, I was surprised to see a "For Sale" sign displayed in a neighbor's yard. Since the lady of the house was out raking leaves, I stopped to chat with her.

In response to my surprise and regret that her house was up for sale she said, "My husband is retiring first of the year and we'll be moving into an apartment."

"Are you looking forward to this change?" I asked, expecting an enthusiastic yes, considering that the relief from leaf raking would be a plus.

"No, not really," she said sadly. "We built this house ourselves fifteen years ago and have accumulated so much. I dread going through our belongings and getting rid of anything. I'm too sentimental, I guess." She wiped a tear from her eye. "Apartments are small, you know, so we will have to sell most of our furniture. I don't know what I'll do with my time, either. But the kids are all gone, so really we don't need such a big place," she rationalized.

I was interested to learn that the decision to sell the house was based primarily on her husband's desire to be freed from yard work, though he was in excellent health and she handled more than half of it.

"I hate to leave my flowers," she said sadly. "I planted over five hundred bulbs last year."

"Does your husband know how you feel about moving to an apartment?" I asked.

"No, I haven't told him," she said quietly. "It's really none of my business. It's his decision." I refrained from verbalizing my utter disagreement and just listened. "With real estate so slow and winter coming," she rambled, "I'm just hoping the house won't sell until spring. No one has even looked at it in the last two weeks, so I'll enjoy it while I can," she sighed. My heart ached to hear of such domestic inequity, innocent as it was.

"Wouldn't your husband care about how you feel about going to a yardless and tiny apartment?" I asked. "Certainly you could compromise and consider buying a smaller house with a smaller yard with room for a few flowers. He won't know you feel this way unless you tell him, and you could save yourself lots of disappointment. You are important and deserve to be happy, too," I sermonized.

With that, my neighbor shot me a suspicious glance. "Are you a women's libber?" she questioned.

"No," I replied, "I just believe in equality and each spouse helping the other to be happy. Open and honest sharing between mates is the only way to achieve this. Your husband deserves to know how you feel."

"I've never heard anything like this," she stammered. "I'll have to think it over."

When a decision affects an entire family or even the other spouse, it needs to be a joint one. Making decisions based on personal, selfish preferences causes problem.

Normal husbands do not mean to mistreat their wives, but some women, mostly over forty, like my neighbor, so afraid of being labeled a women's libber, ignore their own preferences and permit their husbands to unknowingly take advantage of them. Women who deny themselves equal considerations not only gradually lose self-respect but risk developing a martyr complex—"poor mistreated me"—not conducive to companionship marriage.

When a husband realizes that a wife is prone to put herself down or deny herself equality, he can do much to raise her self-esteem by insisting that she air her opinions and feelings through open and honest conversation.

The following situations illustrate how commonly unequal treatment of females occurs.

Understanding Ingrained Superiority

Occasionally one will run across a husband who has been taught to regard women as inferior beings.

Andy often says to Grace, "I'll tell you when I want you to know something." He has convinced her that she does not deserve any better consideration because she is from a broken home, though it was a wealthy one which provided them with a healthy start.

Andy also withholds affection because Grace is overweight. His constant putdowns keep her so emotionally on edge that she is easily overcome with the uncontrollable urge to gorge herself.

"As long as I stay with Andy, I keep a home from being broken, so in that way I avoid failure," Grace consoles herself.

Wrong! Their home is already broken in spirit if not practically. Until Grace recognizes her equality as a human and demands Andy's respect, she cannot help him work through his superiority complex and misconception about her worth.

Fran Brown wrestles with the same type of problem with her husband, Horace. "Horace rarely says anything complimentary. He just expects me to pack his suitcase, keep his clothes clean, put meals on the table, and be ready to entertain with a smile when he brings businessmen home," Fran complained. "Yet, if I ever grumble, he accuses me of being self-centered and ungrateful for how he supports me financially. I feel like a slave. He reminds me of how poor I was when he met me. He says I owe him everything."

Horace suffers from memory lapse, now that he is an executive. He forgets that Fran's nursing skills financed his college education. He lives for his own pleasure—playing golf, skiing, watching TV sports, and expecting sex on demand. He does not buy

Christmas and birthday presents, nor does he care about their relatives or mutual friends.

"What are women for?" he storms. "You think you're something special? Man was created first. Women are to serve men!"

David Mace suggests that the idea that woman is inferior because the first one was made from Adam's rib is balanced by the fact that every man since has been formed out of a woman's body.

Resisting Male Chauvinism

Walter and Monica's marriage was on the rocks. In fact, she had left him and found her own apartment.

"It's women's liberation that's breaking up our marriage," he screamed. "Until Monica got out into the work world, everything was just fine. It's all those divorced women who are a bad influence on her. Tell her to quit work and return to normal," he ordered me in a counseling session.

Walter was resistant to accepting any blame, though he had manipulated Monica since the day he met her. She was fifteen and he was much older. He was in the service and was stationed near her home. He won her heart and allegiance by buying her nice things that her father could not afford and by physically fighting for her attention.

Being the oldest of eight children and having an alcoholic father and a mistreated and bossy mother, made leaving home look attractive. Monica's innocent trust and total dependence fed Walter's male ego and encouraged his chauvinistic tendencies.

Not long after they were married, Walter's true character began to show as he ordered Monica around and expected her to meet his every physical need. If he came home at 2:00 A.M., he selfishly demanded that she get up and fix a meal. He brainwashed her to believe that she deserved no better.

Because she lacked self-confidence and felt financially and psychologically indebted to Walter, Monica kept his physical and verbal abuses to herself. Life was not much different than when she lived at home. If she ever complained, Walter reminded her that she owed him everything. He made her think that she was stupid, uneducated, and inferior to him in every way.

Then, after about twelve years, Walter became so ill that he could no longer work. Shackled with Walter's negative challenge of "You're too dumb to find a decent job" and suffering with low self-esteem, Monica, with fear and trepidation, set out to find employment for the first time in her life.

Much to her surprise—and Walter's—she was hired that first day. In a few weeks she received a promotion. Gradually she realized that people liked her, thought she was nice looking, intelligent, and not inferior as Walter had brainwashed her to believe.

Quickly she gained confidence and self-respect. Almost as quickly she not only resisted Walter's berating attitude but sought physical release from his male chauvinism.

The sad part is that Walter truthfully thought men were superior to women in every way, which

118

said more about him than it did about women. Evidently he had not been around many women.

Though embarrassed by failure, Walter was ready and willing to discuss his marriage problems—even with a woman counselor—if it meant getting Monica back.

But it was too late; their marriage had suffered irreparably. Monica had found someone who appreciated her as a person and treated her as an equal. She would not even consider risking Walter's promises to change.

This story is being repeated over and over as women discover their personal worth and potential and reject demeaning treatment. Normal women do not want to be in competition with men, especially husbands. They just want respect, equal treatment, and freedom to be all they were meant to be.

If a woman will get help when she believes that she is being treated like an object or a possession, her marriage may not only be mended, but salvaged and encouraged to grow into a companionship relationship rather than just an arrangement. I have seen many such marriages survive.

These relationships can be understood, altered, and healed, but not until these men and women understand that God created men and women equally, first for fellowship with Himself and second for a satisfying companionship together.

"Stewardship of Humanity means that we can show appreciation for God's creation by treating others as persons and not things," says Harry Hollis in *Christian Freedom for Women.* "Males should show respect for females by acknowledging the common humanity which links them while also accepting the female's uniqueness. Females can demonstrate respect for males, although, of course, they should reject the continuing exploitation practiced by some males."

Not acknowledging a woman's equality produces the same kind of difficulty within a marriage relationship that using an inferior grade of oil does in an engine. Low-grade oil does not lubricate properly, nor does it protect the parts. The engine is likely to smoke and chug.

12

Approving Spirituality

During these insecure days, materialism, inflation, female role changes, frayed family relationships, increased immorality and fast pace of life pressures are causing more and more women to acknowledge and express their spiritual hungers.

Women, by nature, are more service-minded than men. Paul Tournier says in *A Place for You,* "It is true that women have a greater instinct for service and devotion than men have, and men very often take advantage of the fact. A husband asks for much more support from his wife than he offers her in return."

Many women long to grow spiritually, to attend worship, and to be involved in church activities. They yearn to discover, develop, and use their spiritual gifts as well as to provide a firm spiritual foundation for their children.

Unfortunately, many wives and mothers are not

only confused about female spiritual rights and responsibilities, but they are confronting and battling masculine apathy.

Women's Spiritual Dilemma

Diana Long is frustrated because she wants to serve the Lord, but her husband, Paul, is not so inclined.

"Shouldn't Paul lead out spiritually?" Diana questioned. "I want our children to become strong Christians and our home to be an effective Christian influence in the community.

"I want to have family devotions, but Paul won't cooperate. I don't feel like it's my responsibility to do it, but our children need guidance while they're young. I also want to be in submission and encourage Paul to be in charge, but he doesn't seem to be interested in spiritual matters, though he claims to be a Christian.

"He just doesn't seem concerned about other's relationship to God. I'd love to visit all our neighbors, but he won't go with me. It seems the more I tell him about my opportunities to share my faith at work, the more he clams up.

"Although Paul attends church pretty regularly, I don't think he would go if I didn't insist and get everyone up and moving. Sometimes I think I should just stop and see if he'd take the kids. He considers church and religion my responsibility. I hate to be in charge. What can I do?"

Diana's concerns parrot the problems of many

Christian wives and mothers. They are not afraid of responsibility but reluctant to lead.

Diana considers herself fortunate that her husband is a believer, but her problem is extremely delicate because she wants to experience a shared faith—the epitome of a companionship marriage—with a husband whose spiritual enthusiasm lags far behind hers.

Diana would enjoy teaching a children's Bible class, but the church where she receives the kind of spiritual direction she craves for herself and children requires that Sunday school teachers be members. She does not want to join the church until Paul is ready. Yet she has been waiting over a year.

Diana shares her faith at work, but she is dying to grow spiritually and really get involved in church activities and express herself verbally. But she does not want to pressure or run ahead of her husband. Diana would enjoy a vibrant Bible study discussion, but Paul prefers to sit in a crowded lecture situation where he is reasonably sure that he will not be called to participate.

Is Diana obligated to repress her spiritual longings because she is married to a timid man? Should she put off church membership until he is spiritually and emotionally ready? And should she, who is naturally assertive and comfortable around people, deny her God-given personality and abilities? Or does she have responsibility to obey the admonition of I Peter 4:10: "Each one should use whatever gift he has received to serve others, faithfully administering God's grace in its various forms," whether

her husband joins her or not? Is she responsible for obeying Matthew 28:18–19? "Then Jesus came to them and said, 'All authority in heaven and on earth has been given to me. Therefore go and make disciples of all nations, baptizing them in the name of the Father and of the Son and of the Holy Spirit.'" Was Jesus' command to make disciples of all nations given just to men or to all believers regardless of sex?

Women who wait to satisfy their spiritual appetites and abilities until their husbands lead the way are frustrated. The men may not be listening to the Holy Spirit at all. Why should woman's obedience to God hinge on someone else's commitment? Does God lead all alike? Many women feel trapped between their spiritual conscience and their reluctant husbands. Is that what submission means?

Understanding the Dilemma

Some churches and religious groups regard a woman's personal contribution inferior, or proper only when it is a spinoff of a man's.

This attitude has at last been challenged, thanks to the industrial revolution which has not only forced, but privileged women to set and reach personal, educational, social, and economical goals.

Many women rightly resent that female spiritual rights still lag behind secular freedoms in many churches, making female progress permissible in all dimensions except the spiritual.

The struggle for spiritual freedom dates back to the Reformation which, according to David and Vera Mace in *Christian Freedom for Women*, ". . . did not emancipate women nor destroy the superstitions and tyrannies of former centuries. It did give them enhanced status, and it fostered and nurtured the seed which would grow into a new freedom for Christian women—a freedom to be themselves and to seek directly God's purpose for their lives without having to be dependent upon the directions and interpretations of men."

Women are held at arm's length by many church groups, even though female attendance far outnumbers male. Most churches could not function without female leadership and financial contributions, whether women are directly or indirectly chosen, elected, or allowed to serve.

"The truth is," Harry Hollis writes in *Christian Freedom for Women*, "that many women are forced into these (leadership) roles because of the absence of male responsibility . . . women are not trying to take over society. They are trying to secure basic rights and human dignity."

My book, *Devotions, A Family Affair* (Baker Book House, 1977) discusses in detail why men are often reluctant to lead spiritually, especially at home, and suggests ways wives and mothers can deal with the problem in a loving and creative way.

But, women, whether they are wives, mothers, or singles, are just as responsible for sharing the gospel as men, and need not apologize for their desire to use their talents. Jesus supported women's freedom.

Jesus Was Pro Women

Looking at Jesus' attitude toward first-century women's spiritual potential and responsibility offers a clear and wholesome perspective of what is biblically right today. Jesus did more to release women from bondage than anyone ever has done or ever will do.

Jesus set in motion the attitudes that He knew would progress toward social and spiritual reform, unity and equality among men and women.

In John 8:32 He said: "Then you will know the truth, and the truth will set you free."

In a day when giving birth was considered a woman's greatest contribution and privilege, Jesus countered the statement, "Blessed is the mother who gave you birth and nursed you," with "Blessed rather are those who hear the word of God and obey it" (Luke 11:27–28).

Jesus' dealing with Mary Magdalene in a day when females had little social, economic, or educational freedom dramatized His acceptance and trust in women.

Mary—The Message Bearer

We read in Luke 24:1–12 the account of Mary Magdalene and the other grieving women finding Jesus' tomb empty. The angel there assured them that Jesus had risen. Immediately they took this information to the disciples who were reluctant to believe and accept their report. Peter, however, elected to check out the ladies' empty tomb story.

After searching the tomb and area and seeing, indeed, that Jesus' body was not there, the perplexed disciples returned home (John 20:12). But Mary stayed near the tomb weeping. If the angel's words were correct that Jesus had risen, where was He? Where was His body? By this time her grief was mixed with anticipation, wonder, and expectation. As she bent over and peered inside the tomb once again, she spied two angels seated where Jesus' body had been. They asked, "Woman, why are you crying?" (John 20:13a).

"They have taken my Lord away," she said, "and I don't know where they have put him" (John 20:13b).

Then Mary turned around and saw who she thought was the gardener, and He also asked why she was crying. "Who is it you are looking for?" He asked (John 20:15a).

"Sir, if you have carried him away, tell me where you have put him, and I will get him," Mary pleaded (John 20:15b). She wanted to take care of Jesus' body.

Though Mary had no idea how or what "risen" would mean, she knew something extraordinary was happening. When Jesus said, "Mary," she recognized her teacher and friend. Then Jesus gave her a job. "Go . . . to my brothers and tell them, 'I am returning to my Father and your Father, to my God and your God'" (John 20:17).

Mary obeyed immediately and carried the exciting news, "I have seen the Lord!" along with Jesus' message (John 20:18).

Why Jesus chose to appear initially to Mary instead of to Peter or John, we don't know, but it certainly elevates woman to a place of prime importance and trust.

Paul Was Pro Women

The apostle Paul picked up Jesus' projected spiritual freedom for women as Galatians 3:26–28 verifies: "You are all sons of God through faith in Christ Jesus, for all of you who were baptized into Christ have been clothed with Christ. There is neither Jew nor Greek, slave nor free, male nor female, for you are all one in Christ Jesus." Paul also admonishes in Ephesians 2:10 that "We are God's workmanship, created in Christ Jesus to do good works, which God prepared in advance for us to do."

How can women who wait on men perform those good works?

Women, made in the image of God, just like men, have the same privilege and responsibility of fellowshiping and obeying God through Christ.

All believers—men and women—are made priests and are permitted to enter the Holy of Holies—God's presence—the greatest of responsibilities and privileges. Priests are chosen by God, then given the opportunity to obey. "Therefore, brothers, since we have confidence to enter the Most Holy Place by the blood of Jesus . . . let us consider how we may spur one another on toward love and good deeds. Let us not give up meeting together, as some are in the habit of doing, but let us encourage one another . . ." (Heb. 10:19, 24–25).

Though the Scripture releases men and women

to spiritual freedom, women have struggled since that day for spiritual equality. Frances Anders in *Christian Freedom for Women* states the problem:

> What little freedom and measure of equality were provided women in certain pre-Christian societies was enhanced by the affirming example of Jesus. The early church fathers eventually returned to a pre-Christian position regarding women. . . . The only liberation movement that was apparent in the middle centuries was the growth of conventual groups that gave women the right to choose something other than marriage, numerous children, and subjection to the will of man. Here was the opportunity to choose God over husband; the convent offered a voluntary serviture that brought status and opportunity for personhood not possible anywhere else in that culture.

Fortunately, today, because women have been forced into the working world by either inflation or surplus time, they are finding ways to work through their spiritual dilemma.

Working Through the Dilemma

Let's get back to Diana's "What can I do?" Her counselor reasoned, "You accepted Christ on your own, didn't you? Then, it is your personal responsibility to obey the Lord's commandments and cultivate your individual spiritual growth. Granted, you and Paul should share the load of influencing your children, but your personal growth is your own responsibility.

"Even if Paul, at this time, chooses not to accept his equal share of the family load, out of compassion and concern, you will want to see that the children do not miss the opportunity while they are young to receive spiritual instruction at home and at church."

Finding Her Niche

Diana has to follow the Lord's leading. Assuming that her husband's gift does not match hers, she should not deny herself spiritual expression nor put undue pressure on him. If her sharing about opportunities to witness through the day intimidate him, she should modify her rehearsal of these conversations.

As Diana asks God for direction in sharing her faith, He will lead her in ways that will not antagonize or embarrass Paul. For instance, she can give him encouraging support by agreeing to attend a lecture Bible class where he is more comfortable even though she prefers to participate in discussion. That shows humility on her part—an integral dimension in a companionship marriage.

Humility is helping the other person become the best person he or she can become, always taking into consideration his or her personal strengths and weaknesses and not putting him or her down or expecting that person to become like you.

Submission is synonymous with humility. According to Ephesians 5:21, humility is the basic attitude for all believers: "Submit to one another out of reverence for Christ."

It takes a strong woman or man to be in voluntary

submission. Christ wants the church to be in submission to Him for what He can do for them, not for what they can do for Him. The same is true in a marriage relationship. Each spouse should be more concerned with making the mate's life more meaningful and pleasant.

Though Paul does not care to participate, Diana can get involved in singing in the choir, special studies, and other church activities. She should feel no need to apologize for leaving a couple hours per week, provided her being away is no great inconvenience for Paul. She should treat him as she wants to be treated as Jesus commanded in Matthew 7:12: "In everything, do to others what you would have them do to you. . . ."

Diana can also begin a low-key family devotional period with Paul's involvement his own choice. These adjustments will work only if Diana will risk initiating conversation with Paul and ask God's wisdom as James 1:5 admonishes, "If any of you lacks wisdom, he should ask God, who gives generously to all without finding fault, and it will be given to him."

When Diana overcame her fear of discussing spiritual matters with Paul, she discovered much to her delight that he was not opposed but merely timid about sharing his faith in someone else's domain. He feels very comfortable, however, talking with people about spiritual matters when on his own turf.

Setting and Sharing Spiritual Goals

Since Paul is comfortable and willing to have a couple visit in their home, Paul and Diana decided to invite neighbors whom Diana can ask to a Bible study, which she will also lead.

In her leading, Diana can be sensitive to creating times when Paul can volunteer his opinions and knowledge since he needs a little encouragement to share. Together, then, they can influence others.

By her winsomeness, Diana can bring witnessing opportunities into the home where she and Paul can jointly minister. He will gradually gain confidence and grow spiritually and begin to feel good about his involvement with God's work. Though it is Diana's personality that draws people in, Paul is just as important in reaching out. Diana can assure Paul of her pleasure in his willingness to be a part.

A Christian wife whose husband is not a believer needs to be especially careful not to piously bring judgment and negativism home from church, such as "you should have been there. The preacher preached just what you need to hear: husbands are supposed to be the spiritual head of their homes. Look at you, sitting here fat and lazy in front of the tube."

When the wife returns home from church meetings inspired, more patient and sensitive, and shows her spouse and children more love and consideration, the husband will say to himself, "Going to church really helps her" and to others, as one man shared before he became a Christian, "I like my wife to go to church. When she does, she is a whole lot nicer to me and the kids."

This man was drawn to the Lord because his wife made her personal spirituality and that of the children her own responsibility.

Getting and Giving Needed Support

God never gives a burden for someone or something without supplying both the opportunity and the enabling of the Holy Spirit to meet that particular need. He wouldn't give Diana or you a compassion for reaching out to neighbors, knowing that Paul and/or your spouse would be totally opposed to it.

True evaluation of a husband, according to *The Married Man* by Bob Vernon (Fleming H. Revell, 1980) is how happy his wife is. When our major happiness and peace and approval come from God, needing other's (husbands') acceptance and appreciation is lessened.

Paul Tournier says in *A Place for You:*

> Though knowing others accept and approve of who we are and what we do is the strong support each individual clamors for, human beings can never provide our total needs.
>
> The limitless support which men so painfully lack is to be found only in God. God is always there, always available, and for everyone, both small and great . . . he is the only support on which we may fully rely.

Women are no longer pawns—without choice of where they will go or what they will do. They are persons. When women receive the appreciation they need, they will return more than adequate dividends of encouragement.

Establishing open and honest spiritual conversation encourages a couple to share from the deepest recesses of the heart and mind. This type of communication provides the most stable foundation for growing a companionship marriage. When spouses learn to pray together about their personal and shared concerns, competition, dissatisfaction, and boredom will be replaced with the setting and reaching of worthy goals.

The integral importance of a strong personal and family spiritual life resembles the strategic part the steering gearbox plays in the mobility and direction of an automobile.

An engine in top-notch condition, a crankcase full of clean, quality oil, wheel bearings packed with the right grease, and a transmission filled with fluid do little good if the steering gearbox is not filled with grease to permit smooth and safe movement.

Happy traveling to you!